# JUST SAY...
# YES!

# A STEP UP
# TO SUCCESS

A **14** DAY PROGRAM FOR

PERSONAL ACHIEVEMENT AND BALANCE

# Scott McKain

### with
## Antonia Barnes Boyle

**KENDALL/HUNT PUBLISHING COMPANY**
4050 Westmark Drive    Dubuque, Iowa 52002

# Contents

■ ■ ■

# Foreword

*by Jim Palmer*
*Member, Baseball Hall of Fame*
*ABC-TV Sportscaster*

■　■　■

Even though it has been a few years since I've made a living putting a baseball over the plate, it is obviously something I will never forget how to do. While my mechanics might get a little rusty, or I might not have my best "stuff," the basics have become second nature.

In fact, much of what we do in life has become second nature. We call it habit. Sometimes our habits work to our benefit, but many times they do not. Bad habits are nearly impossible to break.

What should be frightening to all of us is that bad habits can sabotage our goals, dreams, relationships...even our physical and mental well-being.

Perhaps that's the reason I believe in this program developed by Scott McKain, and outlined in this book, **Just Say Yes! A Step Up to Success.** The opportunity to examine your habits, discover your priorities and develop a plan for positive action is one you should not pass up.

I honestly believe this program really works. It is all about getting what you want...and wanting what you get...in life. The way I see it, that is what really counts!

Read this book, do the exercises Scott suggests, implement the plan of action you develop, and "Just Say Yes!" to your dreams and yourself!

# Introduction

■  ■  ■

Life should not be as hard as we have made it.

We can...as strange as it sounds...simplify our lives and enhance our success at the same time. At the risk of sounding like those trite old sayings in many self-help books, you really *can* live the life you truly want to live.

The purpose of this book is to show you *how*.

With that, it is my pleasure to welcome you to the **Just Say Yes! — A Step Up to Success** program.

There's more than a welcome and introduction here. I also want to say, "Congratulations!" When you selected this book, you showed me that you obviously believe in the type of positive action that you need to take if you're going to make your life better and your accomplishments greater.

It is an old maxim that a journey of a thousand miles begins with one step. The problem is, however, that so many people never take that solitary, initial step. You *have*...by beginning this program.

Another point to make here at the beginning is that you are going to read ideas in this book that you may have previously encountered elsewhere. I am convinced that is positive and important.

First, my goal in this book is to present the best information, material and ideas (no matter who originated them) so you can design your life to be more successful, dynamic, and enriching than you ever thought possible.

And, second, while some of the information may appear somewhat familiar, I believe the way it is presented, organized, and arranged is unique. This book will enable you to develop your individual system for success. Robert Fulgham had a similar approach when he quoted the French writer Montaigne in his book, "Uh-Oh."

The essence of Montaigne's understanding is that while it might be that someone else has grown the flowers, the art of the florist is arranging the individual flowers in a way that "ties them together in a bunch."

I believe there have been wonderful and enlightened ideas in the field of human potential for the past 2,000 years and more. My job for this book is to take those concepts and "tie them together" in a bunch that will be unique...and be the catalyst that helps you move yourself to reach and exceed your potential.

Throughout this book, you'll find that I'll be asking you to answer specific questions. We'll go through the questions together and then I want you to stop and write down your answers. It is best if you use a separate notebook or binder that becomes your **Just Say Yes!** Workbook. In this way you can develop your own resource manual that will assist you in taking a step up to success.

After you have completed answering the questions, return to this book, and we'll talk about what your responses mean.

Here are the questions I want to you to be thinking about as we begin the program:

■ **Number One:** *If your life could be everything you want — if you could do what you want to do, have what you want to have, be who you want to be — what would that life be, exactly? Specifically, what would you have? Precisely, what would you do?*

Are you one of those folks who thinks, "Well, I'd just like to be happier. I'd just like to have things easier," or do you want to know exactly and precisely what you're going to do?

■ **The Second Question is:** *How has who you've been in the past affected who you are today? How is who you are today going to contribute to who you want to be in the future?*

The old adage is: The past is prologue. In other words, what has happened to us in the past is what we can expect for the future. The philosopher, George Santayana, said: "Those who cannot remember the past are condemned to repeat it."

Have you ever stopped to take a look where you've been so you can get some kind of idea where you're going?

■ **The Third Question I'd like you to answer is:** *What level of commitment do you have to make certain the future is better for you?  How committed are you to ensure that the future becomes everything you want it to be?*

Take as long as you need to answer these questions on your worksheet. When you're finished, we'll get started on the **Just Say Yes!** Program.

# DAY 1 Ourselves and Our Commitments

Do you have the questions answered? I'll bet it wasn't as easy as you thought it would be.

However, be encouraged by the fact that when you answered the questions, you took the first step up to saying "yes" to yourself and saying "yes" to the things in life that you want! You were taking a step up to success and taking the positive action necessary to make great things happen for you.

Before we review the questions I just asked you, let's examine a little about how the answers will help you in the development of your personal **Just Say Yes!** Program. As you know, this program is a fourteen day commitment on both our parts: yours and mine.

Your commitment is to do the exercises and assignments that I ask you to do...and don't go on to another day's tape before you've completed the work you need to do from the day before.

You're going to be identifying and replacing old, non-productive habits. You'll be discovering your strong inner forces — the priorities that direct your actions. And, you'll learn how to realign them with the specific, realistic goals you'll learn how to set and achieve.

We're going to be talking about the importance of your daily actions and how understanding your personal action style has an impact upon everything that you do. We'll talk about the best ways to communicate your needs and wants to others so they become your partners instead of your opponents as you work to achieve your life's ambition.

Finally, we'll examine each of the six specific steps up to success that you need to take. These are six direct actions that will change your life more dramatically than you could have ever envisioned.

And, we'll do it all in fourteen days!

Just two weeks out of a lifetime.

So that's our bargain. It is our commitment to one another.

You do the inner work necessary to understand yourself and set your goals; I'll give you the steps you need to take to make your life rich and fulfilled.

Now that we understand each other, we'll review the questions I asked you earlier.

In this exercise, the answers are so personal that I'm not going to spend much time discussing them, but I do want you to understand that they will be part of the skeleton that supports the rest of your program. They tell you about you...and there's no more valuable information you could have. You'll want to think about your responses often.

■ **The First Question that I asked you to answer was:** *If you could do anything you want to do, be anything that you want to be, what would it be?*

Let's say money is no object. Where you live, your physical size, your age and education don't matter.

Because I want us to focus on specifics during this program, I want you to dream a little and be very definite about how you would like your life to be if you were in total control. There are many books and tapes and seminars that talk in great generalities about becoming a better person or becoming the person you want to be...but many of them never get specific.

That's one trap we're going to avoid.

We're going to look at some of the specifics you're going to accomplish and then develop a precise game plan.

I compare it to top-notch baseball or basketball or football coaches. You don't hear them say: "Well, let's just go out there and play as hard as you can. We'll just hope for the best!"

Not a chance.

They develop a game plan.

They *expect* that you're going to play hard, but they also map out the specific moves that will get you where you want to go so you can win.

I would like to think of myself as that kind of winning coach. I'm here to help you develop your game plan...to help you think through what action steps you need to take to lead you to success.

■ **The Second Question I asked you was:** *How has the past has contributed to where you are now, and how is what you're doing now going to contribute to where you want to be?*

I think it's very important that we understand that everything we've been through has brought us to where we are today.

To a great degree, we've become a society that exists by making excuses.

We want to blame someone or something else for where we are now. We're very quick to point out that the reason we haven't achieved what we want to achieve is because we came from a dysfunctional family, we've been the victim of prejudice, or other people stopped us from getting ahead.

Now, I'm not saying all of these situations do not actually happen.

Of course they do.

But, the point is, we can't let excuses prevent us from living the kind of life we want to have.

My challenge to you is to stop leaning on all those excuses you've used as a crutch up to this point!

I want you to analyze them in a professional, intellectual, detached manner — as if they were someone else's excuses and not yours. You've got to be willing to take full responsibility from this moment on for your future — that responsibility is one of the keys for success in this program.

■ **The Third Question was:** *What level of commitment do you have to make sure that life is better for you?*

Well, I trust you have a fourteen-day commitment. I earnestly hope that you will seriously commit to working on this program for just part of each day for the next fourteen days to enhance and enrich your life.

You may think that fourteen days sounds like a lot of time so let's put it in perspective. On your thirty-fifth birthday, you'll have been alive just about twelve thousand, seven hundred, seventy-five days.

What have you accomplished in that time? I'm only asking for a small part of each of fourteen days so you can turn your life around. It's not too high a price to pay.

That being said, I'm going to ask you to answer another question.

■ **Here is Question Number Four for the first day of the fourteen day program cycle. On your worksheet, *write down five clichés that your parents — or other significant people — filled your head with while you were growing up.***

Let me tell you one my Mom told me (and I'll bet your Mom told you), "Don't go out of the house without wearing clean underwear...you might be in an accident!"

Haven't we all heard that? Naturally, I thought if I happened to be in an accident serious enough for the doctors to have to cut off my pants...my underwear wasn't going to be clean anyhow!

I want you to think of five declarations like that — five statements that may or may not be true — but that you grew up hearing all the time. Write them down now.

Take a look at your list of five statements and see how many of them are negative.

So many of the things we are told as children *are* negative.

Don't leave food on your plate. Don't run with a lollipop in your mouth. Don't cross the street. Don't hurt animals. Don't pick on younger kids. Don't talk to strangers. Don't take candy from someone you don't know.

They're all positive directions but they're expressed in negative ways.

I believe that what all this negativism did was condition us toward negative responses!

We've heard "no" often from the time we were born until today. For instance, I was in a restaurant the other day and the sign in front said: "No shoes. No shirt. No service." Opened up the door and on the cash register was a sign that said: "No credit cards." I walked to my seat in the "No Smoking" section. I opened up the menu and it said: "No baked potato until five p.m. No substitutions allowed." The waitress walked up and said: "May I help you?" and I said, "I don't know if you can!"

We hear "no" so many times that we're conditioned to what we can*not* do. I was told so much about what I could not do that it took me a long time to discover what I really *could* do.

And, that's the whole point of **Just Say Yes!**

Some studies say that the average fourth grade child has heard the word "no" (or other form of negative message) over seven hundred thousand times.

If you divide the nine years that child has lived by the number of times they've heard "no," it comes out to 77,778 times a year. Or two hundred thirteen negative messages every day.

Take it one step further. Let's say the child is awake an average of fourteen hours a day, that's roughly fifteen times an hour the average child hears the word "no." If you've raised a child, you found out "no" is one of the first words out of your darling's mouth. Why? Because they hear it so much!

What is more disturbing is that while a nine-year-old has heard "no" seven hundred thousand times, he's only heard "yes" about one hundred thousand times in that same period.

In other words, we hear "no" seven times for every one "yes" that we hear.

With that preponderance of "no's," is there any reason to expect that we're going to react in a positive way when we're so conditioned to the negative?

Of course not.

If you still need more proof, turn on your television. Is there any doubt about what we hear?

The positive is placed at the very end of newscasts in what journalists call a "kicker story." It's just a little something to make you smile at the end of twenty-seven minutes of horrible news. You've heard all the bad stuff, now here's a little candy coating so it tastes better.

In newspapers, the happy items are dropped in as a paragraph at the end of other stories so there isn't any white space. They call them "column fillers" and no newsroom takes them very seriously.

Even when you hear the weather forecasts, the meteorologist will announce a "thirty percent chance of precipitation" rather than a "seventy percent chance of clear skies!"

One of my missions in this program is to reintroduce you to the word "yes."

But don't misunderstand me. I'm not suggesting you say "yes" to everything. I'm not suggesting you say "yes" to every whim, every circumstance, every idea that comes along.

I don't want you to overdo it.

I am suggesting that we need to change our initial reaction to situations that are presented to us from the negative and turn them into positives.

I'm suggesting that one of the most important actions we can take is to learn is how to say "yes" to the opportunities around us and to say "yes" to ourselves.

What happens too often is we say "no" to ourselves but we still say "yes" to everyone else. After a time, that leaves us angry and frustrated and unwilling to take any action. That's when the inertia sets in and our lives start going in circles — which gets us nowhere.

What we have to do is focus on ourselves and focus on the "yes."

I would suggest you cannot "no" your way to success. You cannot "no" your way to the life you want to lead.

The ads for the number one athletic shoe company in the world, Nike, don't say: "Just *think* about it" or "Just *hope* for it" or "Just *wish* for it." The ads say: "Just *do* it!"

In other words, there's a positive action — a "yes" — involved there and it makes all the difference in the world.

When I pick up my Bible and look in the New Testament, I can't find a single book called "Hopes" or "Wishes" or "Dreams" or "Discouragements" or "Wants!"

But, there is a book called "Acts."

To me, there's nothing sadder than someone who's given up "doing" in favor of just "being"...someone who's "existing" instead of "living."

One of our goals for this first day of the fourteen we're going to spend together is to have you focus on what your past has made you to this point in your life.

Has it made you negative? Have your experiences made you think about what is NOT working right in your life?

I don't want to be as simplistic as the cliché about the glass being half empty or half full, but I do want to open you up to the possibility that when we change our perspective, we change our attitude.

Not too long ago, I was asked to give a speech in Hawaii. As long as I was there, I took a little extra time and lay out by the swimming pool at the hotel.

A grandmother came out to the pool with her grown sons and their families. They all took their places on the pool chairs and one of the sons turned to his mother and said, "Mom, we just can't believe it. This is one of the first times you've ever been out on the beach when you didn't have one of those motivational books with you."

You can believe that got my attention since I'm in the motivation business. So, I listened very carefully and heard the mother say, "You know, I've read just about every one of those books that I could ever find and I've never found one yet has made my life any different."

Wow! That really hit home with me. To think that someone could have read all that information and still it hadn't changed her life.

Then I heard her other son laugh and say: "But Mom, you've got to do more than just read the books."

"You've got to do something about it."

That really hit home with me as well.

It's not going to be enough for you to just read this book.

It's not going to be enough for you to just spend a little bit of time over the next fourteen days being a passive participant.

Even when you've completed all the course work I'm going to give you, even when you know yourself perhaps better than you ever have before, it's still not enough.

You've got to get off your...er, couch...and go do something about it.

You see, many of us have been spectators at our own lives. We haven't changed anything for ourselves because all we do is just "keep on keeping on." And, the challenges for us are to find out what we can do to make things different...and better!

Thinking about that, there are a couple of other steps we have to take on this first day.

I don't want to spend too long talking about myself, but if you're going to trust me with your future over the next two weeks, you should know a little bit about me.

I'm not a movie star and I'm not a millionaire.

I'm not even very famous outside my own circle of clients, friends and family.

However, there are some pretty important things I do have.

I have a successful career, financial stability, and a wonderfully happy marriage. I have lots of fun and I lead a great life.

The reason I'm telling you this is because I want you to know that I practice what I preach.

I've helped many, many other people attain the same satisfactions in life I have and I can help you attain them as well.

I grew up in the very, very small town of Crothersville in southern Indiana. If you saw our television program, you saw a little bit of my home town. You could also have seen parts of it in the old John Cougar Mellencamp rock and roll video "Small Town."

That's where I spent my childhood.

When I was growing up, it was assumed that I'd either stay home and farm or I'd take over the family grocery store. Of course, there were a couple of problems associated with that.

Number one, there was someone older in our family that was going to get the farm.

Number two, I hated working in the family grocery store.

Yet it seemed that everyone would try to restrict my opportunities to those two limiting choices.

When I entered high school, I talked to the guidance counselor about the courses I should take. I found he had already signed me up for the courses *he* thought would be best for me, since I was naturally going to work on a farm and sell groceries. He had just assumed that I'd follow in my father's footsteps.

Don't misunderstand me...they were great footsteps...but they weren't on the path I wanted to take.

I think that it's a real shame that we try to make young people choose the course of their lives so early on — and then structure everything they do to meet those criteria we've set for them.

Studies show that of the new entrants into today's workforce, about half will end up retiring from jobs that have not yet been created.

It's amazing! We have no idea what the future holds, and yet we try to restrict someone's options.

I was very lucky. I didn't have to accept my guidance counselor's plans for my future because I got involved in the FFA — the Future Farmers of America.

The FFA gave me exposure to information I wouldn't have been able to obtain any other way at that point, and in that place in my life.

FFA taught me about how to set goals and make choices, about how to set priorities and about how there are trade-offs in anything that you do.

It also gave me the chance to be inspired and motivated.

I believe all of us need that.

While I was learning all this during my high school years, something really very important was happening. I was beginning to understand there is a *system* we can use to approach life the way it should be. I was learning that we can become even more than we ever dreamed we could become. I was discovering that opportunities are there no matter who we are or what we've done in the past.

And, I found out that no matter where we want to go, we can find a way to get there.

But, another very important thing happened to me along the way. There were goals that I'd set for myself in the FFA that I *didn't* accomplish. I flat lost out on them.

For instance, I wanted, more than anything, to win the State FFA Public Speaking Contest. It was my top goal throughout high school. This was want I really wanted.

My freshman year I entered, and was defeated. "No big deal," I thought, knowing I had three more times to try.

My sophomore year, I entered and, in preparation, gave my speech to seven different civic clubs and organizations in my home area.

The result was the same, however,  I lost again.

Deciding I just HAD to win in my last two attempts, I entered the contest a third time the following year.  I gave my speech to seventeen civic organizations.  Again, I failed.

My senior year...my final opportunity to achieve my top goal in high school, I entered the competition.

Months before the contest, I wrote and polished my presentation.  I practiced my talk in front of over twenty audiences. I practiced so much in my bedroom, my parents had my speech committed to memory.

I practiced in the barn lot.  My COWS had the speech memorized!

I went to the contest, gave my speech...

...and I finished dead last.

As you might imagine, I was crushed.  For a while.

Even though I didn't achieve that goal, if I hadn't pursued it so vigorously, I realize there is no way I could be doing what I'm doing now.

You will find out, as we go through this program, that there may be goals you set that you don't achieve but your life will still be better because you pursued the opportunities!

Sometimes you'll find you're better off even if you don't get everything you hoped for.  You'll still get more than you would have if you hadn't tried.   Success won't always come easily — and it shouldn't.  If it's too easy, then everybody would be living an enhanced life and it would have no value.

Before we conclude today, I want to discuss how much times have changed and continue to change every day.

I know I'm not telling you anything you don't already know. We're seeing changes in our work lives and in our professional lives. I know in every organization I've dealt with, on every job site I've visited, there are enormous changes occurring.

It seems that every employer wants more done with fewer resources.  That's a definite change.  The boss wants higher productivity but he gives you fewer resources to accomplish it.  We need more productivity but many organizations aren't willing to admit they have to spend more to get it.  These are times of pressure and change in the world of work. The pace has been accelerated. Time is money, so there must be an accounting for every minute.

There are technological changes, too, especially in the workplace.

If you look around you, I'm sure you see technology changing. For those of us a bit older, we've seen the progression from typewriters to word processors to desktop computers and mainframes. Whole departments have been replaced by a machine. Whole job categories have disappeared. Highly skilled workers, like linotype operators at newspapers, have had to learn the computer or find another trade.

Information is the name of the game and we add new words to our dictionaries ever year — audio cassettes, CD-ROM, CDI, satellite conferencing, video phones — every day we have new technology to master. No sooner do we learn one machine than it seems that here comes another to replace it.

In addition, we've seen changes in how our professional lives fit into the overall scheme of things.

For example, perhaps you have been involved in a lay-off, or a "R.I.F." (reduction in force). Maybe you've seen it where you work and it may have made you less confident of your future than ever before.

I remember it wasn't that long ago that you would join a company as a young person and fully expect to get your watch or pin or ring signifying twenty-five, thirty or forty years with the same organization.

The company was your extended family and they would take care of you, and you would work the rest of your life for that company and retire with a pension. That was just the way it went. It worked that way for your Dad and your Grandfather, why not for you? Today, you see all the lay-offs and changes and plant closings and you wonder if you might be next.

Maybe you're doing very well and you just want to do better, but because of this change, you have less control in your work.

The change is happening *to* us, not *with* us.

As a result, we find ourselves less in control and less satisfied with what it is we do.

And, change is happening personally too. This has, perhaps, even more of a dramatic impact. We've seen changes around us as everything seems to cost a little bit more, and we seem to have a little bit less at the end of each pay period.

We see the economic pressures that the government is facing in health care, Social Security and foreign trade (to name a few), and we realize that we are the ones who are going to have to pay the bill.

Our personal lives are a little bit faster paced and less fulfilling because we have less quality time together with our families. Many homes now depend on two paychecks and there are enormous pressures that accompany that — especially when there are kids to care for.

We've seen other changes in our personal lives...the videocassette recorder and the microwave oven and cellular phone and on and on. Technological changes are affecting us at work and they are having an impact on us at home, too.

The result is the same process happens at home that happens at work. We become increasingly pressured and dissatisfied. We never feel we've achieved enough because we're always playing "catch up."

When we're talking about change and the changes that we're going through in our lives, there's good news and bad news.

The bad news is, change is constant. We're always going to have change.

It's bad news because most of us don't take advantage of the changes so we can say "yes" to new opportunities. These are the people stuck in a rut, and the cumulative effects of today's changes are going to make it even more difficult for them to deal with innovations in the future.

In other words, the more things change, the tougher it's going to get for people who don't adapt and who don't take positive action.

The good news is: change is constant. We're always going to have change.

The good news is that change is going to be constant, because whether you like change or not, you can develop a strategy that can help you stay in control of your lives in these unstable times.

I strongly believe most of us want life to be more than what we currently have. I don't think any one of us is completely satisfied with where we are in life, no matter how much we achieve. For instance, if you were totally satisfied, you wouldn't have bought this book to better your life.

Satisfaction is nothing more than a fancy word for inaction.

When we're satisfied, we don't grow. When we're contented, we don't change. We just stay put. I want to be happy, but I never want to settle for being merely content. I want fulfillment, but I never want total satisfaction.

Starting over twenty years ago when I was with FFA, up to this day, I have had the chance to talk with successful people all over the world. I've met political leaders including the President of Brazil and three Presidents of the United States. I have talked with movie stars and celebrities and top business people.

Do you know that not one of them expressed total satisfaction with what they had achieved?

I have yet to meet anyone who says: "Well, that's it. I'm going to quit now. I'm completely satisfied with every aspect of my life."

The main attribute all successful people have in common is that we all want life to be more than it is, no matter how much life currently seems to be. The challenges of the future are so important that when we stop facing the future, we start to die.

It doesn't matter what age we are, it doesn't matter how much we've achieved...there's still more out there for us.

Let me tell you about the fellow I was sitting next to at a banquet when I was 21 years old — Colonel Harlan Sanders of Kentucky Fried Chicken fame.

During dinner, Colonel Sanders asked me if I knew where he'd gotten the seed money to develop Kentucky Fried Chicken.

I figured he must have had an investor but he said no, it came from his first Social Security check. I've never forgotten that.

It's never too late, it's never too soon. You're never too smart, you're never too dumb. You're never too rich, you're never too poor to take advantage of the changes in your life.

However, the question is: How can we move past all the negative conditioning we've had over the years of change and begin to say "yes" to ourselves?

Here's your assignment for Day One of our fourteen day journey.

It's easy to get caught up in the changes and challenges and do what we've always done and only seek gratification in what has already happened.

I want to suggest to you that what we need to do is to start out by noticing some things. There are two assignments I want you to complete before you begin reading tomorrow.

First, I want you to do something to say "yes" to yourself.

It's not something extravagant or something silly or stupid but it's something out of the ordinary.

I don't want you to go overboard and buy a car or anything that grand — but I'd like you to buy yourself a new shirt or a new blouse, or pick up and go to dinner and a movie in the middle of the week.

Say to yourself, "Yes, this is something I want! This is something I deserve!" Go out and do something you wouldn't ordinarily do to say "yes" to yourself.

Then, about an hour or so later, what I want you to do is write down how you feel about that experience. How do you feel now that you've spent some money on yourself or taken some time for yourself and said "no" to someone else?

I want you to be very observant and tune into your reactions and feelings.

Second, I'd like you to answer a question I first started asking back in the mid 1970's. It is not a new question...it has been asked over and over by speakers, authors, and other "insight givers" in one way or another for years. Most recently, Dr. Stephen Covey, author of "The Seven Habits of Highly Effective People," has been using a similar question with great impact.

What I would like you to think about and do is imagine, if you will, that your time on earth is over and you're looking down at the eulogy presented at your funeral.

You're listening as someone talks about what your life meant, what it was all about — not only in terms of your accomplishments but also in terms of how you affected other people.

Before you read the next chapter tomorrow, I want you to write your own eulogy. Take some time to think about it. Then, write down on your worksheet what you'd like to hear at your funeral if it could be exactly what you would want it to be — and if you had lived the life that you wanted to live.

I don't know if newspapers are still doing this, but one of the privileges of fame — if it can be considered that — was being able to edit your own obituary. Some newspapers would send obituaries to world class celebrities to make sure that all the facts were correct and well-reported.

Wouldn't it be illuminating to know what they were going to print about you after you died?

Most of us don't have that option...so I'm giving you your chance to look back on the life you would want to have remembered.

In our next chapter, we'll take a look at what you've written and begin to build your personal **Just Say Yes!** process, so you can step up to success.

## DAY 2 | Habits, Values and Priorities

This is the day we're going to start talking about the three focal areas around which our lives revolve: our habits, our values, and our priorities. You'll understand how you can undermine your dreams and goals if you don't recognize each of these three elements of your persona.

You'll learn why you need to go with the flow instead of swimming upstream — and why you'll never change your life for the better if you can't align what you want with how you feel about life.

First, I want to take a few minutes so we can go over the exercises I gave you yesterday. I hope you took the time to answer the questions.

If you skip even one step in this fourteen day plan, you'll upset the program balance, a balance that's needed to redefine and redirect your life. If you didn't do the exercise — if you didn't say "yes" to yourself in some concrete way and you didn't write your own eulogy — then please stop and do it before you read any further.

Yesterday I asked you to say "yes" to doing something for yourself that wasn't your normal routine. What did you do?

Did you buy yourself something? Did you treat yourself to lunch or dinner in a nice restaurant? Or, did you order in just so you wouldn't have to cook?

If you're a busy Mom, maybe you hired a sitter for a couple of hours so you could lock the bathroom door and pamper yourself with a bubble bath and a good book.

Or, maybe you're a guy who's had your eye on a new putter

and now it's in your golf bag.

It really doesn't matter what you did or how much you spent. The important question is: Was it difficult to do without bringing someone else into the situation?

For instance, if you went out to dinner, were you able to eat it alone or did you have to bring somebody else along? If you bought yourself something, did you also have to spend some money on your spouse or children so you wouldn't feel guilty?

In other words, was it difficult just to say "yes" to yourself?

It *is* difficult for a lot of us. Many of us are conditioned that it's okay to say "yes" to everybody else but it's not okay to say "yes" to ourselves.

We're going to change that attitude during the next two weeks.

You're going to learn the art of selfishness — in its best sense. Unless you know and love yourself, your life is at a standstill. There's no way you can move forward.

So let's understand each other.

Even if you share it with someone, this program isn't about anybody else.

It's about you.

As we go through the program, please don't compare your responses with how someone else might think, or how you feel they'd react to your answers.  It's okay to focus on yourself for fourteen days.

Remember, you've already been on this planet for thousands and thousands of days, probably spending most of them worrying about everyone else.  Taking a couple weeks to concentrate on you won't hurt.

In fact, I know they'll help.

As we go along, I'll bet you'll find that the better you get at saying "yes" to yourself, the better you get at saying it to other people, too.

So, think about it now:  Were you able to say a guilt-free "yes" yourself?

Your second assignment was to write the eulogy for your own funeral.  What did it say about you?  How was your life explained? What was mentioned as being important to you?

Isn't it amazing how our priorities change when we think about how we want to be remembered?  Did you talk about your contributions to your friends, family, and community?  Did you talk about the importance of the relationships that you've had?  Did you refer to the organizations that knew you as a volunteer and the people whose lives you'd changed in a positive way?

Sure you did.

What didn't matter anymore is which banks you dealt with or what kind of car you drove or how many houses you owned.  All the material aspects of life become pretty meaningless when put in the perspective of a funeral eulogy.

And, that's exactly the reason for this exercise.

One of the things that often happens when we talk about success is that we talk in terms of money, material possessions, and the power that we wield at work.

When we prepare a eulogy, however, we skip over all that and talk instead about how the deceased had an impact on the lives of other people.

Status and prestige are expressed not in terms of the amount of money in the bank but what was done with the money to realize personal goals and benefit other people.

Isn't that interesting?

In the very first part of this book, when we were talking about having anything we wanted,  most of us tended to answer that we'd like to be happy or we'd like to be rich.

When we start talking about what we'd want our eulogy to be at our funeral, however, we talk more specifically about what sort of parent we were, what sort of spouse we were, what kind of person we wanted to become and what kind of success we hoped to attain.

I want you to keep these points in mind as we go through the goal setting exercises later in the book.

The more specific you can be about where you want to go in your life — the more specific the system for success you will develop for yourself.

While I was writing this book, a very dear friend of ours called to tell me that her significant other, with whom she'd lived for a number of years, had died suddenly.

They'd given a little dinner party Saturday night, and had a wonderful time. The next morning, they realized there wasn't any milk for cereal. My friend ran out to the grocery store and returned home a few minutes later to find her companion dead.

No warning. No previous illness. No pre-existing medical condition. Just dead of a heart attack at forty-seven.

In many ways, that's just about as tough as it gets.

As we talked a little about the challenges she has to face now that she's alone and her life has changed 180 degrees, it occurred to me that she's going to find a great deal of difficulty dealing with some of her habits. The comfortable and accustomed patterns of her daily life aren't ever going to be quite the same again.

I remember a widow who told me what she found the hardest for her was to pour two cups of coffee in the morning, and then realize there was only one person left in the house.

Mothers often awaken in the middle of the night to make sure the kids are home safely — even though their children are all grown and off on their own.

The point is: The power of habits is incredible.

Someone dies or moves away and we continue the patterns we've set. Habits control the way we live. We do today what we did yesterday — and the day before that and the day before that.

There have been many books written and theories advanced about why we act this way.

I'm less concerned with the psychology and inner motivations of what we do than I am with our actual, measurable, observable behavior.

For instance, have you ever noticed at work that it is always the same people who tend to run a little late getting to their desk? You know who's going to arrive cheerfully in the morning and who will be grouchy and have a rough time getting started.

In other words, the morning people are always the morning people. The late runners are always the late runners. The grumps are always the grumps, and so forth. Our behavior tends to be remarkably consistent and that's because we've fallen into patterns of habit.

When we bring those habits face-to-face with the changes that we talked about on Day One, we see there is a potential for real conflict in our lives.

It is precisely that conflict that is the barrier separating us from success.

I had breakfast at a coffee shop not too long ago and a very attractive waitress came over to serve the coffee. I said, "Well, how are you doing this morning?" She said, "Oh, not too well, but what can you expect? It's a Monday."
"Oh really, " I said, "Mondays are bad?"
"Mondays are always bad," she said.
So I asked her what happens after Monday and she said, "Well, it just kind of tapers off after that."
Obviously, because this person was directed by her habits, she expected Mondays to always be bad. She was probably also a member of the Thank Goodness It's Friday club. Monday's are to be dreaded and the other days taper off after that.
How much satisfaction do you think she's going to have out of her life? Not too difficult to guess, is it?
Her negative belief habit had become a self-fulfilling expectation.
The trick is to change our habit of dreading Monday to one of eager anticipation for a new start, to change our habitual expectation of failure to one of savoring the win.

As I mentioned yesterday, right now, we're going through a time of fundamental change in our society, both in lifestyle and livelihood. This is a change that's causing a revolution in terms of how we think and how we want to live our lives.
It's a more dramatic time for our nation than we really understand.
I believe that...in its own way...it is even more dramatic than what the Japanese learned after World War Two.
After the war, the Japanese made the conscious decision to take their nation from rubble to riches. I'm old enough to remember when the phrase "Made in Japan" meant junk.
Today, "Made in Japan" means quality, especially if you're buying electronic equipment.
The Japanese went through a fundamental social and economic change at that particular point in their history and they turned their country around.

In the United States, we're going through a change that's equally fundamental.  As a society, we're changing how we want to live our lives.  Our priorities have shifted.

However, since we're not in the horrific situation Japan was back in 1945,  the changes we're going through are a little tougher to detect.

When you combine the changes in our priorities  with the established habits of our daily lives, all of a sudden many of us are running into conflict.  Let me give you some specifics.

*Men's Life* magazine recently reported that sixty-three percent of the men interviewed had revised their life's ambitions to give their marriage a higher priority than making their fortune.

Sixty-three percent!  It's a phenomenal statistic.

Think of the male stereotype.  As men, we were raised to go out and conquer the world, make more money than our neighbors and be more successful than our classmates.

We smiled indulgently when we heard "The only difference between men and boys is the cost of their toys."  Our motto was: "The guy who dies with the most toys wins."

Now,  sixty-three percent of us are willing to change our life's dreams to put marriage before career.  The relationship is going to come before the Porsche.  Saturday chores will replace golf with the guys.

This is becoming an age of sensitivity.

In May of 1993, California state senator Gary K. Hart announced that he wouldn't seek reelection because he didn't want to be an absentee father.

Television newsman, Ted Koppel, put his career on hold a few years ago, to be a stay-at-home father while his wife completed law school.  Books like Robert Bly's "Iron John" are trying to put men in touch with their softer, more sensitive nature.

That is just a tiny sampling of what's happening.  This is the era when children can divorce parents who aren't fulfilling their responsibilities.  Women are finding their capabilities are unlimited.  There's "a brave new world" out there that's changing more rapidly than novelist Aldous Huxley ever dreamed when he coined that phrase.

Now, the good news is there are workable technologies we can use to help us develop a system for success within our changing structures. We can get more and do more and be more and love more and live more than we ever have before.

We can do it by changing our thinking along with our habits.

Habits are one of the most powerful influences shaping our lives.

The English poet, John Dryden, said: "First we make our habits and then our habits make us."

In fact, many addictions are reinforced by habit. If you've been a smoker and tried to quit smoking, you know first-hand how difficult it is to break a habit. And, I'm not talking about nicotine. That's a chemical drug addiction. For smokers, one of the hardest things is to find something to do with their hands. To stop raising that cigarette, lighting that cigarette, going through the physical movements of smoking is the hardest adjustment to make. It's a physical action that smokers make without thinking about it.

Here's a simple test to show how changing our habits will make us uncomfortable.

Fold your arms across your chest.

Look and see which arm you have on top. Now, on the count of three, reposition your arms so the other arm is on top. Ready? One — two — three.

Feels awkward, doesn't it?

You probably took both arms apart and had to think about it before folding your arms the other way. It feels awkward because we are such creatures of habit that we always fold our arms the same way.

I read one study that said that sixty-two percent of people have always, throughout their lives, put the same arm on top. They've never even done what you just did and tried it the other way.

Here's another test.

Fold your hands, interlock your fingers, and see which thumb you have on top. Now, on the count of three, take your hands apart and reposition them so they interlock with the other thumb on top. One, two, three. Doesn't that feel unnatural?

Habit controls us so completely that we fold our arms the same way every time. We fold our hands the same way. We live our lives the same way.

One of the real challenges that we're going to have to break through in the next few days is to take a constructive look at what our habits are. Then, we must objectively analyze how to replace the ones that have trapped us in unproductive patterns of behavior.

Here's what I'd like you to do for the first of today's exercises. I'd like you to stop and try to think through and analyze what an average day might be for you.

What are the habits that define your life?

Eating habits. Behavior habits. Smoking. Nail biting. Watching television. Things that you do day after day after day. Write down as many daily habits as you can think of that you exhibit in your behavior day after day. I want you to take the time to do it properly so stop now and fill out that part of your worksheet.

What discoveries did you make about your behavior?

As you went through the process, did you notice, for example, that you usually have a hamburger and French fries every day for lunch? Why?

Because it's a habit. It's easy to go through the drive-through. Or, maybe it's your habit to over-sleep because you always turn off the alarm. Have you formed the habit of exercising every evening after work — or is it your habit to come home and flop on the couch in front of the tube?

Did you notice anything that you do over and over and over when there's no particular reason why you should?

It's like the great mathematician, David Hilbert, who was known for being both very absentminded and very set in his ways.

One night, guests were coming over for dinner and his wife noticed he needed a clean shirt, so she sent him upstairs to change. After about half an hour, she went to check on him and found him lying in bed asleep. You see, Hilbert was a creature of habit and after he took off his coat, his tie and his shirt, he was used to getting into bed and going to sleep.

Now, our habits may not be that strong but I'll bet a lot of them are. I know they're very, very difficult to break.

If you don't believe it, tomorrow morning try putting your right shoe on first instead of your left. Try changing any mindless habit. It's hard to do.

Here's the problem...while most habits are harmless, some habits are extremely limiting.

It's said that insanity is doing the same things over and over again — and thinking you're going to get a different result. What happens is that we do the same things over and over because it's comfortable because the action is familiar. Then, we go through life hoping for different results, not realizing that our habits or actions have to be different as well.

The question, then, is how do we change these habits? You can't just stop a bad habit. You have to replace it with another — hopefully better — one.

Just try to change the bad habit of an incorrect golf swing if you want to understand what a challenge it can be. The secret is to keep practicing the new behavior until it, too, becomes a habit. As Denis Waitley says, "Practice makes permanent."

I've found that the only force that can cause us to truly change our habit patterns is the priorities that we have established in our lives.

Our priorities — those aspects of our lives that we put the most value on — are stronger than our habits and they are the only tool we have to help us change.

Unfortunately, priorities are one of the most important yet least discussed keys to our future success. During the next couple days, you'll have the opportunity to discover your priorities and how to use them to work for you in reaching your goals.

I've talked to a lot of people in the past twenty years and I'm always struck by how unsatisfied the average person seems to be.

These people aren't at the bottom of the pile trying to get up. Some of the most successful people I've ever met have told me they wish they could feel better about themselves.

People with big money. People living incredible lives. People whose names you would recognize are asking this question: "Why don't I feel better about myself and my life?" It's like Peggy Lee's classic song, "Is That All There Is?"

What people are really saying is that whatever they've achieved, whatever they've earned, it doesn't satisfy the needs deep within them.

Why do we do the things we do in our lives?

Habits are just manifestations of deeper-seated tendencies. They rise out of our values and priorities.

Values are the very most basic rules by which we live.

The fact that we have a conscience shows that we have values. Patriotism, religion, honesty, charity, ethics — these are all values that we live by. We have them instilled in us as we grow up and they stay pretty much the same during the average person's lifetime.

One of the questions that many people will ask when determining values is: "What would you die for?"

The most common answers have almost become clichés. "What would I die for?" Obviously we'd die for our kids, we'd die for our spouse and our parents. We'd die for our country and, in many cases, for our fellow man.

We can say that and we can smile and feel good because we know that we'll probably never have to make any of those heroic gestures.

Frankly, I'm not very interested in what you'd die for because our goal is to talk about the positive actions that we're going to take so you can say "yes" to yourself. That's what's important.

For me, the real question is: What are you willing to live for? How would you like to live? What do you stand for? What won't you stand for? In other words, we change by choice — so what are you willing to choose to believe in?

We've all heard so much about the importance of having values, about family values, about values as they relate to business, that sometimes we get away from what values really are. If we look in a thesaurus for words that are similar to "value" we find synonyms that really relate more to money, words like "price, cost, worth," and "benefit."

I believe value really relates to what we believe in without reservation, to the things that we hold most true.

I believe that our values are our anchor in life, keeping us stable just as an anchor keeps the boat stable at the dock or at sea. We don't have to think about values very much. They're just there — the moral foundation for everything we do.

These deep-seated values — like the Ten Commandments and the Golden Rule — are what keep talk show hosts in business. We tune in to watch the people who pore out the sordid details of their lives because how they live is in direct opposition to the values we cherish.

People whose values are different from ours are aberrations and we find them an endless source of fascination.

The same holds true at the office. When businesses get away from their value systems, they lose sight of why they exist. These are the kind of businesses that serve their needs first instead of providing benefit to their customers.

You've seen the kinds of businesses I'm talking about: Hospitals that are more worried about getting paid than helping the sick. Car repair operations that are more concerned with warranty than repair. Computer departments that are more centered on selling new hardware and software than helping customers understand the systems they already have.

It becomes very, very important to understand that in business and at home, values serve as our basic grounding mechanism.

What I'm saying is that you can't truly utilize the strength your values give you if you don't understand what they are.

Philip Selznick, writing in the book, *Leadership and Administration*, wrote: "The institutional leader is primarily an expert in the promotion and protection of values."

That's a leader in an institution.

I think the individual leader is primarily an expert in the acting out and protecting of and the refinement of their own personal values.

Somewhere between our habits (which we can change), and values (which we usually don't), you'll find our priorities.

Priorities are those areas of life that we consider the most important to our personal fulfillment. When something is a top priority, we give it our full attention.

However, too many times we put the priorities in our life on the back burner during the process of earning money and success — and that's where we start encountering roadblocks.

A lot of motivational and self-help programs that talk about goal setting, time management, and living a better life, really don't begin where they should — at the beginning.

They don't begin by examining what our priorities are.

That's too bad. If we listen to them, our priorities can be the most powerful, positive, and productive forces in our lives.

It's important for you to understand that we're not going to make any judgments on this program. It's not my place to tell you that one set of priorities is any better than any other, that there is any one particular way that you should feel.

However, it is my goal to make certain you realize that *you* have to choose the direction of your life, and that's a choice that *only* you can make. And, by the way, not making a decision about where your life is headed *is* a decision. It is deciding not to decide...it is choosing a lack of direction. It makes as much sense as buying a boat without a rudder.

Another point to remember is that priorities are not static. They can — and do — change throughout your life.

Just because you grow up with a certain set of priorities doesn't mean that they won't change. What's most important to you at twenty will probably not be equally important when you're forty-five.

People who have been through this program tell me that one of the most profoundly affecting parts is identifying, examining, and evaluating their priorities.

You may decide to make some changes or alterations. That's positive. You may feel stronger than ever about your priorities and decide to keep them just as they are. That's positive, too.

We're going to examine your priorities so you can take a good, hard look at what's most important to you.

Now, what I'm suggesting to you isn't psychology. We're not trying to examine *why* you feel what you feel. Instead, we're trying to get out of the excuse mode, to stop making excuses for the past and get on with the future, moving towards saying "yes" to a productive life.

You'd have a lot of trouble driving a car if you only looked in the rear view mirror. You've got to look ahead to get where you're going. And to look ahead in your life, you have to examine where you are and what your priorities are.

Look again at that eulogy you wrote and you can see some of the areas where your priorities might lie. For instance, if part of what you've talked about was being a great parent, it would seem that family is probably an area of top priority. If career success is what you have concentrated on, that's probably another important area for you.

Whatever you said in your eulogy will be a revelation of where your priorities might be.

You'll find, as we look at these priorities, that they may be in conflict with what you do every day. This is where the self-defeating conflict comes in. If we're going to be priority-directed in our lives, instead of habit-directed, we're going to have to understand our priorities in greater detail.

My father was a good example of how our priorities and habits can be in conflict. Dad loved his family. He was happiest when he could get us kids together and go out on a family outing. But, he was brought up with a stern work ethic so he worked long hours in his store. Except for planned occasions — or when we were working for him after school — we didn't see much of him.

Then one day Dad had a heart attack. Now, when that attack hit, do you think Dad was wishing he could have had more time at the store or working on the farm?

I don't think so.

It was the warning that taught Dad the importance of listening to his priorities — to spend time with the family he took such good care of. If he hadn't been at odds with his inclinations, maybe the stress wouldn't have hit his heart so hard.

Just as an organization or a company would have a mission statement about the reason for that business to be in existence, our priorities are really our personal mission statements. They are the things that are so important to us that they weave the fabric of our lives. When we get away from our priorities, we're never going to be as happy as when we're following their pattern.

If you live in harmony with your priorities, you're going to be happy. Even if you're not successful in terms of the monetary things you want to achieve, you're still going to be happy because of the integrity with which you've pursued achievement.

People who live in synch with their priorities tend to be more successful than people who don't. There's a passion and an integrity about the way they pursue what they want in life.

They lead lives that are so much more significant and so much more productive than those people who are simply chasing the almighty dollar or doing what they think they should be doing instead of what they want.

There are varying levels of importance that we place on the priorities that we have.

Some are of primary importance.  Some are not quite as significant.

What we are going to do is find out what your priorities are.

Your assignment for Day Two is to begin the process of isolating and understanding your priorities.

The following pages are a test on personal priorities.  It will allow you to score in each of six dominant priority areas: Enlightenment, Individualism, Structure, Power, Altruism, and Economics.  During the next two days, we'll talk about each of these priorities in greater detail.

Some of you are going to be uncomfortable with this because priorities aren't something you can touch and feel.

Others aren't going to want to go through this process because you feel you don't need the structure of this sort of exercise.  You want to do it your own way.

Some of you will love the test because it *does* have structure.  You know what you're supposed to do.

As you'll see, that says something about what is important to you in terms of your priorities.

I cannot overstate the importance of going through this exercise to pinpoint your personal priorities.  I truly believe that if you are not living in concert and congruency with your priorities — and through them, your values — then you are not going to be successful and fulfilled in life.

It's a basic foundation, a fundamental principle, of learning to just say "yes" to yourself and developing a system of positive action — so you can step up to success.

To be successful, to be an achiever, to be fulfilled and enriched, you have to find out what drives you, what moves you personally and professionally.

There is no doubt, what will move you are your priorities.  They alone can give you the strength and commitment to override your habits.

I don't want you to think that it's too late to begin to change your habits and bring them into alignment with your priorities and values. It's never too late.

More and more we're hearing about middle-aged executives who give up their briefcases and three-piece suits to return to a small town where they can open a store or run a bed-and-breakfast or work as a laborer.

People are beginning to realize that life is too short spending it doing something they dislike — just because they chose it when they were eighteen and had to declare a major in college.

Many people feel suffocated because their habits box them into achieving things that don't fulfill their priorities. If you fall into this category, there are a couple of reasons you might feel trapped.

First, perhaps other people have told you what your priorities are.

Maybe you have a high priority in one particular area that you started to express when you were growing up. Then your parents or teachers told you it was wrong to feel that way so you changed to conform to someone else's pattern.

This is important to understand. Your true priorities may have been sublimated to what you were told you ought to believe and how you ought to live your life. When you realize where your real priorities lie, you will instantly see what is really important, what you really want out of life — and the most effective way to get it.

Another reason you might feel trapped is because while you're achieving, you're achieving outside your priority activity — like the renegade executives. Perhaps you have become more concerned with earning a living than making a life.

I know of one case that involves a very good friend who's a CPA, a certified public accountant. She has her MBA from a top university. She was on the fast track with a good job in a solid company — and she gave it all up to be an aerobics instructor.

Sound strange? Maybe, but now she's very, very happy. While going through the process, she found out that she hates the world of accounting. She doesn't like structure. Financial goals aren't that important to her. She was more concerned with being able to express her individualism. As a C.P.A., she wasn't having her priorities met through her actions.

I believe priorities are behavior initiators. They are what began our behavior towards a successful life. They're also hidden motivators. We can use priorities as a way to motivate us to find the success that we want.

Priorities can also be hidden *de*-motivators. They can turn us off. They can keep us from being successful when our actions take us in a different direction that our priorities lead us.

We're going to get a handle on this during the next two sessions after we discover what your specific priorities are.

As you take the test, please follow the directions carefully and when you start reading again tomorrow, we'll begin to talk about three of the six dominant priorities that give focus to our lives.

Give some thought to which priorities influence your personal life and your professional career. They could be very different — or they could be the same.

■ ■ ■ Personal Priorities Test ■ ■ ■

For each of the following situations, rank your highest preferred activity as "1"; your second choice as "2", continuing with your least desirable option as "4."

Do not think too much about your responses...just answer the questions quickly. Your initial response provides the greatest indicator of what you really think and believe.

1) What quality is most important in a friend?
   __ a. sincere concern for the welfare of others
   __ b. a willingness to stick to commitments
   __ c. a desire to learn more about you and the world around us
   __ d. a dynamic personality that influences others

2) If these seminars were offered in a local hotel, which would you attend?
   __ a. HOW TO ENHANCE YOUR INVESTMENT RETURN
   __ b. HOW TO WIN IN ALL NEGOTIATIONS
   __ c. EFFECTIVE VOLUNTEERING TO TRULY HELP OTHERS
   __ d. DO-IT-YOURSELF BUSINESSES

3) What would you like most about a job?
   __ a. A well-defined set of expectations of performance
   __ b. The opportunity to set your own rules
   __ c. The chance to learn and become an expert in your field
   __ d. The potential for unlimited income

4) If you were going to enroll in a class, which would you select?
   __ a. "Philosophy & Religion From a Scientific Perspective"
   __ b. "Economics in a Personal and Professional Context"
   __ c. "Dominating the Scene — How to Succeed in Company Politics"
   __ d. "Examining the Needs and Opportunities of the Disadvantaged"

5) Rank the importance of the following statements in order:
   __ a. "While I care about others, it is most important for me to take care of myself. If I don't, no one else will. If I'm not happy, I can't make anyone else happy either."
   __ b. "We must enforce the rules of society. They are here for a reason. Just because something is new doesn't mean it is better. If we are going to change, it should be in an orderly fashion."
   __ c. "Life is a continual learning process. We should constantly seek to stretch by reading, listening and examining. There is so much out there to continue to learn! There are so many ways in which I can grow."
   __ d. "We are placed on this earth to help others. What defines us as a person is how much we give of ourselves to assisting others. Our primary commitments should be to our families, our friends and to others."

6) In which order would you read articles about these topics?
   __ a. Time management
   __ b. Upcoming changes in interest rates
   __ c. Creating more freedom in your job
   __ d. Leadership secrets of corporate CEO's

7) Who would you select to work with?  Someone who is:
__ a.  smart
__ b.  compassionate
__ c.  has authority
__ d.  organized

8) Which of these rights are most important to you?
__ a.  personal freedom to do what you want
__ b.  freedom of worship and religious expression
__ c.  economic freedom
__ d.  right of society to establish laws and regulations

9) The greatest reward of success is:
__ a.  being able to help others
__ b.  making money and enriching your life
__ c.  being the boss
__ d.  getting to do what you really want to

10) Number your priorities in life from 1 (most important) to 6 (least important)
__ a.  **Enlightenment** — the need to learn more, intellectually or spiritually
__ b.  **Individualism** — the need for personal freedom and independence
__ c.  **Structure** — the need for routine and security
__ d.  **Power** — the need to influence others and be seen as a leader
__ e.  **Altruism** — the need to help others, even at one's own expense
__ f.  **Economic** — the need to obtain and maintain financial security and achievement

**Scoring the test:**
There are six basic priorities in life.

Below are the answers that correspond to each of the basic priorities.  Go back to the test, and write down the scores you gave the answers identified below.  Then, add your scores for each of the priorities.

For example, the answers that relate to the Enlightenment priority are "c" of question 1; "c" of question 3; "a" of question 4, "c" of question 5; "a" of question 7 and "b" of question 8.  To obtain my

Enlightenment score, I'll go back to question 1, and write down my score for answer "c"; then, answer "c" of question 3, and continue for all scores for each of the answers listed. Then, I'll add all six scores to get the total score for that priority. Continue these steps for each of the six basic priorities.

Enlightenment answers: 1c/3c/4a/5c/7a/8b
Scores you gave these answers:___ ___ ___ ___ ___ ___ =
Total Enlightenment Score:

Individualism answers: 2d/3b/5a/6c/8a/9d
Scores you gave these answers:___ ___ ___ ___ ___ ___ =
Total Individualism Score:

Structure answers: 1b/3a/5b/6a/7d/8d
Scores you gave these answers:___ ___ ___ ___ ___ ___ =
Total Structure Score:

Power answers: 1d/2b/4c/6d/7c/9c
Scores you gave these answers:___ ___ ___ ___ ___ ___ =
Total Power Score:

Altruism answers: 1a/2c/4d/5d/7b/9a
Scores you gave these answers:___ ___ ___ ___ ___ ___ =
Total Altruism Score:

Economics answers: 2a/3d/4b/6b/8c/9b
Scores you gave these answers:___ ___ ___ ___ ___ ___ =
Total Economics Score:

On this test, the lowest score is the highest priority. (Just as in golf, the lowest score wins!) The second lowest score is your second most important priority, and so forth. List your priorities in order, from highest to lowest priority. (Remember, this would be the lowest to the highest score. The lower score is the higher priority in your life.) If you have tie scores on some priorities, use question #10 as the tie breaker to determine which is most important. But, use question #10 ONLY as the *tie breaker* and not as the sole authority on your priorities.

As you examine the results of this test, you may have discovered a difference between what you assume your priorities are (the answers to question #10), and how your values and inner feelings are directing you (the scores from the answers to the other questions).  As we progress with this program, you will discover the importance of "Just Saying YES!" to your values.  To step up to success in life, we must follow our value-orientations.

**Your Priorities in Order:**

# DAY 3 | The First Three Priorities

Please review your assignment from yesterday in which you took the test on personal priorities.

You'll notice that you have a score in each of six areas. We're going to tell you a little later on how the scores relate to one another, but first let's look at each score individually. Over the next couple days, you'll understand a lot more about each of these six priorities and how the order in which you rank them impacts your life.

It is essential to be clear, from the very beginning, **we are not making value judgments.**

In other words, it's not my job to say that one priority is better or more important or more substantial than any other. It's certainly not my intent to say that one is right and another is wrong.

Even though I have my own opinions, these are based on the way that I live and on *my* personal priorities, and I could never assess what's right for you.

What *is* my job is to help you find what's important to you so you can help construct your own system for success, through priority-directed living.

As you look at the your test, you'll see that you scored higher on some priorities than others. Today, we're going to look at the first three of the six core priorities.

What we want to keep in mind is that our value-driven priorities are important building blocks for success. In order to be enriched, we have to live our lives with congruency, with harmony, and with wholeness.

That means we can't live our lives as a pretense. We have to be true to the activities that we consider most important.

To get started on aligning our priorities with our goals, we need to understand what those priorities are.   Simply explained, priorities are the propellants that make us want to do the things we do.  They are perspectives from which we look at our world...the spin that we put on the activities in our lives.

For instance, we all have some degree of each of the six core priorities that we're going to be talking about — Enlightenment, Individualism, Structure, Power, Altruism, and Economics.

We all want to make money, be respected, and help make the world a better place.  We want to live in a society that has laws but we want to be king in our own castle.  And, we have a constitutional right to be informed.  Each of the priorities has an impact upon us in one way or another.

Where the real synergy happens is when we look at our priorities ranked in the order of their importance to us.  Then we begin to understand how they can enhance or impede our success.

For example, Joe and Bob both want money so they can pay their mortgages, support their families and put food on the table.

Joe, however, wants just enough money to feel secure and be able spend his free time volunteering his services to community organizations.  The Economics priority isn't that important to him, but the Altruism priority is.

Bob, on the other hand, might feel that money will bring him the material things he wants in life and it will give him the opportunity to be in control of his destiny and the destinies of other people who depend on him.

Bob's Economics priority is very strong — as is his need for Power.  Helping other people — Altruism — may be much farther down on the list.

The disparity in our priorities is fine.  It is not only what makes us different from each other — it's what keeps our society on an even keel.

If everyone wanted to be a general, there wouldn't be any troops to carry out the orders.  If everyone wanted to be a scholar, there wouldn't be any industry to pay the light bill at the library.  It is a system of balances.  To be really successful, you have to establish the individual priority balance within yourself and work with it instead of against it.

Let's start by talking about what I've arbitrarily called Priority Number One: Enlightenment. Please remember, there is no reason to believe that any one of these priorities is any better than another so the order in which I talk about them has nothing to do with their relative importance.

The first score that you have on your worksheet represents your interest in Enlightenment. The Enlightenment priority is the driving force in people who place a high emphasis on knowledge for the sake of knowledge — on learning as a core value.

These are people who are naturally curious about the way their world functions today and in the past. These are people who are searchers. They like to study.

People with a high Enlightenment priority place great value on intellectual gain and the theoretical approach to knowledge. They want to study to find the truth — whether it's scientific truth, practical truth or philosophical truth — they are deeply concerned about educational growth. Learning is the most important thing they do. You might say they have "*In*quiring" minds instead of the "*En*quiring Minds" served by the tabloids.

People who feel that learning about their spirituality — and investing time and effort in growing from a spiritual viewpoint — are some of the folks who place a high priority on Enlightenment. They're searching to expand their base of knowledge.

When I say "spiritually," that doesn't mean that they have to be religiously oriented, in terms of looking for a divine meaning of life. It also doesn't mean that they have to be intellectually oriented, consistently defining the universe in terms of facts and figures.

The drive that propels the Enlightenment priority is a person's need to search for more knowledge than they currently have, not because it's part of their job, not because it's important to how their family lives.

They want to feed their spirit as well as their body. People with a high Enlightenment priority pursue knowledge simply for the reward within themselves that they get from learning.

Dr. Charles Jarvis has been a speaker on the professional circuit — and one of the great ones — for over a quarter of a century. He comes from San Marcos, Texas, and was a dentist for a number of years before he got into the speaking profession. Charlie Jarvis told me that he has awakened at four a.m. for the last twenty-five years.

Why? By getting up at four in the morning, he can get four hours of solid, quality study time in before the rest of the family gets up around eight o'clock.

He exemplifies the person who places such a high priority on Enlightenment that he's learning — just to learn.

The Greek philosopher, Plato, said: "The life that is unexamined is not worth living."

You can bet that Plato had a high Enlightenment priority. He understood that the more you learn about life, the less you know — and so you keep studying.

In fact, in one of the ancient Greek academies, the students were put through three years of training. The first year, they were called "the wise men." By the second year, they were called "the philosophers." In their final year, they were called "the learners."

The learners in our society are the people who stop what they're reading to look up the exact meaning of a word. Their home decorating plans revolve around the bookcases. When you take a volume off the shelf in their library, you find it's been well-read. There are probably underlined sentences and notes in the margins.

These are the people who take advantage of their city's museums. They know the local librarian by name. The bookstore owner brightens noticeably when they come in because these are the people who buy books — lots of them.

Naturally, everyone has some interest in Enlightenment, but most of us don't have it to the extreme of becoming a mini-expert on one subject after another.

The people who have a lower Enlightenment priority tend to get their information from headlines and television news programs. They need to be informed, not educated. They read *USA Today* and *Reader's Digest* instead of *The New York Times* or *Wall Street Journal*. They'll choose the condensed version of a book over the unabridged — and probably made it through college literature classes with a *Cliff's Notes* and the classic comic versions of the books on the reading list.

They continue to operate within their current base of knowledge. The person with a low degree of Enlightenment is the person who isn't really that curious by nature.

There's nothing wrong with you if learning isn't the most driving force in your life. The Dr. Jarvis's who get up at dawn to study for the joy of it aren't in the majority.

However, I would suggest that if you're reading this book, in some degree you have a significant Enlightenment priority. Part of the reason you bought this program was to learn something about yourself and how you can live the kind of life that you want to live.

Here are a few questions to help you get a little bit further into understanding where your level of Enlightenment is...

After you read the questions, I'd like you to stop while you answer them and return to the book when you're finished.

■ **Question Number One:** *What was the last book (other than this one) that you read simply for fun?*

■ **Number Two:** *How much of the reading and learning that you do is "trashy" novels...as opposed to information that might be stimulating intellectually or spiritually?*

■ **Number Three:** *If there were one subject in the world that you could know more about, or would like to know more about than you currently do, what would it be?*

Stop and answer the questions now.

Let's take a look at your answers to those three questions.

The first question is: What was the last book you read for fun?

The reason we ask that question is that some people can't remember the last time they read a book, let alone what it was. Too many of us graduate from high school or college and figure we'll never have to read a book again. That's very sad.

There's a speaker who inspires me a great deal and his name is Charles "Tremendous" Jones. He says: "There are only two things that are going to impact your life — the people you meet and the books you read."

The books that you read and the people who you meet will have a great impact on your life. If you haven't read any books, then the fact of the matter is your life probably hasn't changed a great deal from the inside out.

Try setting as a minor goal for yourself to find a book and read it.

Question Number Two asked:  How much of what you read is trashy as opposed to informational?

I read a recent column by humorist Dave Barry who said he must have been talking so much that he missed the announcement on the airport loudspeaker.  Looking around him, he figured that no one was allowed on the plane if they didn't have a copy of a John Grisham book.

It's so true.  The unofficial boarding pass of the early 1990's seems to be a Grisham book in your hand.

John Grisham is the author who had three best-sellers on the New York Times Best Seller book list the same week.  He's written *The Firm, The Pelican Brief, The Chamber, The Client*, and *A Time to Kill*, among others, and all of them are extremely popular.

I know, I've read them all — and if you're looking for a fun read, pick one up.  Or choose a Tom Clancy thriller or a Danielle Steele romance or a Judith Krantz story or a Steven King tale of horror.  They're all great page-turners and they make the time pass quickly.

However, if popular novelists are the only thing that you read, then you're really not stimulating your need for  Enlightenment.

Pick up a current biography or a book that will help you develop professionally — or make you a better partner in your relationship or a better parent to your children. Check out your local bookstore to get a self-help or a psychology book, a book on business or management styles, a book on personal development, even a book on geography about some part of the world you haven't yet visited.

It's like giving your intellect a shot of vitamins.

I've got to be honest here.  It's okay to read the popular stuff. I do and I thoroughly enjoy it.

But if it's the only thing you read,  it's much like only eating junk food.  You have to balance your reading just as you balance your diet so you can be mentally and physically healthy.

The third question is:  If there is one subject that you'd like to more about, what is it?

Every answer is going to be different, but as you look at your response, ask yourself: Why haven't I learned more?

We're all filled with excuses: "Well, I just didn't have enough time. I couldn't afford the classes. I don't know where to find information."

The fact of the matter is, if we turn off the television for just thirty minutes a night and read, it's amazing how much more we'd know about the world in which we live — and how much that we could learn about areas that interest us.

Think about it! Thirty minutes a day for 365 days is 182 and a half hours! You can learn a lot in that amount of time. And if you keep it up, studying only one subject for five years, you will have spent 912 and a half hours on it. As the great American motivational philosopher Earl Nightingale pointed out so often, you can become an expert at anything if you study it for just five years!

Let's go on to Priority Number Two. Individualism.

People who place a high priority on individualism are people who value personal independence. They need to be in control of themselves and the situation. They don't want to take orders from other people. People with a high degree of Individualism place a high priority on their own uniqueness, on being able to live the way they choose to live.

Entrepreneurs are a perfect example of this. Their choice is to go their own way and march to the beat of their own drummer. And that's vitally important to these people.

For example, somebody who'd place a high value on having a job where they don't have a supervisor constantly looking over their shoulder would be exhibiting a high degree of Individualism.

I work a lot with salespeople regarding how to stay motivated so they can achieve their goals and get what they want out of life.

It's interesting because most sales managers tell me that salespeople are primarily motivated by financial gain.

I don't believe that to be the case. I've met as many salespeople who are motivated by the independence that goes with the job as I have who stressed the amount of money they could make.

A lot of people place a high priority on this freedom at work. It's very, very important to them, not just as something they think they'd like but as a real gut-level need. It's internal and intrinsic to the way they choose to live. If they can't have an individualistic lifestyle, they feel claustrophobic, as if they are boxed in by unseen walls.

The people with Individualism as a priority are often highly creative and introspective. They don't mind being alone and need their space. Children often show these traits when they are the only child in the family. They aren't team players. They'd rather work overtime and skip lunch than work with others who'll challenge their decisions.

The other side of the coin is the person with a low Individualism priority. These are the people who become uncomfortable when left alone. They need people. They need to be a member of the team. They don't want to take responsibility for their own actions. They like the relative anonymity of being part of the group. These are the chorus members, not the soloists.   The thought of eating a meal alone in a restaurant is intimidating. They'll talk to a stranger just so they can share the time with someone.

Now that you understand more about the Individualism priority, here are three questions for you to reflect on.

I want you to put down the book while you jot down the answers on your worksheets, and then return to the reading material after your answers are complete.

- ■ I'm going to reveal my age a little bit with the First Question.  Remember the old Anacin commercial where the daughter screamed:  "Mother, please! I'd rather do it myself!"  I want you to think about the last time you said: "Never mind! I'll do this myself!"  *Try and remember the last time that you chose not to delegate but to handle a project on your own.*  If you've never done that, when was the last time you *didn't* do it?

- ■ The Second Question is:  *How much time do you spend by yourself?  Is it by choice or is it just the way it has to be?  How do you feel about being with yourself?  When you are alone, do you feel comfortable?*

■ **Question Number Three:** *How would you feel about starting your own business? Or, if you have your own business already, what was the determining factor that made you start it?*

After you've answered these questions, please return to the book.

Let's talk about the questions. Question One was: When did you last say "I'd rather do it myself?" If you had a hard time remembering the last time you said that, you probably place a low priority on Individualism. You prefer being one of the crowd. But, if you can remember a lot of times when you said "I'd rather do it myself," perhaps you have difficulty in delegating to other people. Perhaps your own Individualism is so much a part of your make-up that you want to make sure that you do everything alone.

People with a high degree of Individualism are, on one hand, pioneers — and on the other hand, they're people who don't want to deal with other folks. Sometimes, they want to do everything on their own, almost to the point of alienating the people around them.

Question Number Two was: How much time do you spend by yourself and are you comfortable doing so? There are some people who really look forward to getting private time, time away from everyone else, time to be by themselves.

Then there are other folks who have a low degree of Individualism and they have a rough time entertaining themselves. They don't want to eat alone. They don't want to be alone at anytime. Obviously, there are extremes on either side of this priority. People who want to be by themselves all the time sometimes need to look at enhancing and developing greater social skills. If you like people with you constantly, you might need to evaluate your level of self-confidence. Find ways to do projects on your own to heighten your Individualism. It can be as simple as building a model airplane or putting a puzzle together. Do something alone so when it's finished, it can give you the sense of pride and accomplishment that you might need.

The Third Question I asked you was: "Would you start your own business? If you have started your own business already, why did you do so?"   People with a high Individualism score will say the main reason they started their own business was because they wanted to be their own boss. They didn't want anyone else to tell them what to do. Entrepreneurs with a little bit lower score tend to reply: "Well, I wanted to pursue the American dream" or "I wanted the financial opportunity" or "I wanted to be in charge."

It's interesting that entrepreneurs don't always have high individualism scores and I think we can see that in the number of new businesses starting up every year.

Franchises, for example, or multi-level marketing organizations, have enjoyed a great degree of success, not in small part because they provide a support group. This way less individualistic people don't have to be alone.

Now, let's move on to Priority Number Three:  Structure.

People who value Structure are folks who want to do the "right" thing.  If Structure is your highest priority, you are most comfortable functioning within the rules, supporting established protocol and standards.

I'm not trying to build a stereotype, but a good example might be someone in the Marine Corps.  If you ever saw the movie, *A Few Good Men,* you'll remember there were characters who were very, very rigid in terms of Structure.  It was the structure that gave them strength.  Following the rules was important because they felt the rules are what gives their individual lives — and their society — a great degree of order.

People who place a high priority on Structure expect others to support the standards as well.  They're good at quality control and attending to detail.  These are people who never let their daily organizer out of their sight because they know there's a time to get up and a time to work and a time to play and they don't want to miss one of them.

And interestingly enough, the people who place a high priority on Structure don't feel imprisoned by it.  Instead, they feel Structure liberates them and gives them freedom to live.  It's the organization, discipline, and detail that contribute most to their fulfillment in life.

Structure is one of those values with a wide degree of variance from individual to individual.  You probably know some people who are incredibly structured, who can't do anything without checking their watch and calendar. You know other people who have no structure whatsoever. They just seem to drift about in different directions, letting the wind blow them in where ever it chooses.

What I hope you see evolving through this discussion of priorities is that we tend to assume the way we are is the right way — but it may not be the right way for our neighbor.

Most people that I know who have a high Structure priority have a low degree of tolerance for anyone who isn't organized. And the other way around. I think that those of us who dislike organization — and I admit to placing a very low priority on Structure — often look at highly structured people as being too rigid and uptight. I hope during the this program that we're going to become is a little more open-minded about why other people do the things they do, as we discover what drives each of us to action.

Not having a lot of Structure, I always wonder where this priority comes from? Are we born with it? Is it something that we learn? Is it something that we emulate because of people we admire? If our parents insist on structure when we're little, do we continue that pattern throughout our adult lives — or do we consciously break away from it?

Let me give you an example from my own house. As I've told you, I'm an entrepreneur. I don't like office routines. I like to get up on my time and work when I feel like it. I want to be in control of my own destiny.

My wife, Sheri, used to work with me and my habits drove her crazy. She wanted to establish schedules and routines. She wanted to designate a place for everything in the office and keep everything in it's place. I couldn't find anything unless she was there.

Finally, we saw the difference in our ways and she left my employ with no regrets and went to work in a large corporation. There she's in an important management and marketing position. She goes to work at the same time every morning. She has her day fully organized. She works out almost every evening before coming home. You can almost set a clock by her schedule.

She's happy in her Structure — and I'm happy without it. We truly have a great relationship.

One of the actions you should take is to examine how much Structure you need as an adult. How important is Structure to you in your priority system? Look at other ways to experiment to see if you'd like to increase or decrease your level of priority in the Structure category.

Now it's time for you to answer three questions on Structure. As before, after I've read the questions, please put down the book, and write your answers on your worksheet.

- **Question Number One:** *What is your daily, normal schedule? What time do you get up? What time do you eat lunch? What do you do when you get to work? Is there a specific bedtime? Are there television shows you never miss or certain hours every day that you're sitting in front of the tube, no matter what's on? What is an average day like for you? How much Structure is there for you in that daily schedule? Describe it!*

- **Question Two:** *Which are the three areas in your life where having a set schedule helps you and how does it help? Where is Structure a positive in your life and where does it have a negative effect?*

- **Question Number Three:** *What are three sets of structured rules where you work?* And after you write those rules, I want you to think about them for a little bit. *Are the rules that you've selected good? Are they bad rules?*
  *Are they rules that are neither good nor bad but they're just kind of meaningless or silly? Do you like them or do you resent them?*

Take all the time you need to answer these questions and we'll discuss them after you return.

In the first question, I asked you to outline your daily schedule. There are a couple reasons that I did that.

The first reason was so you could see how difficult it is for you to write down what you do every day. People with a high Structure priority tend to have less difficulty with this exercise than people who don't place much priority on Structure. If you have a high Structure value, I'll bet you found you know your pattern pretty well. You know how what time you get up and how long it takes to get dressed. You can tell us what time you leave the house and how long it takes to drive to work and so on.

If you have a low Structure value, you tend to be a little bit more flexible: "Well, usually, I do this but if I don't feel like it, I may do that. " You had to think about it just a little bit more. People who put a higher priority on Structure tend to have a longer list than those with a lower Structure priority.

The second question I asked was: Which are the three areas in your life where having a set schedule helps you and how does it help? Where is Structure a positive in your life and where does it have a negative effect?

If you examine your answers, they might give you some insight about how much Structure you have and where some areas for improved balance might be.

If you think that Structure is the backbone of your day, you want to try to loosen up a bit and not be so rigid. Be more spontaneous.

If you see areas where the lack of Structure hurts you, you might want to try to firm up your organizational skills and your time commitment.

The third question I asked was: What are three rules where you work? Are the rules good, bad or silly?

One of the reasons that we ask this is that employers impose rules on us...just like *we* impose rules on our *lives.*

Our priorities, values and habits are nothing more than rules that we've imposed on ourselves. Unfortunately, we seldom take the time to examine our personal rules as closely as we do the rules imposed upon us at work.

We're imposing rules upon ourselves that limit our creativity, limit our freedom, limit our financial success. One of the actions we have to take through this process is to examine our priorities so we can change those that are negative, un-productive, un-fulfilling and non-empowering.

This is also a time to admit that some of your self-imposed rules may be just plain silly.

Every so often, a newspaper will print lists of ridiculous laws that are still on the books somewhere. You can't step on a crack in the sidewalk. You can't ride a horse on Main Street after midnight. You can't walk barefoot in public. You know the kind I'm talking about.

We laugh at these laws but many people have equally stupid rules that they've imposed on themselves — silly structures that we force upon ourselves — because of an unexamined priority value system.

You must eat dinner at six o'clock. You can't drink soup out of a cup. You always sleep on the right side of the bed. All sorts of unimportant structures fill our lives.

If you recognize what your priorities are, they will be the foundation upon which you build your goals. Your daily actions will be directed towards the results you want. But, if you're operating from a shaky foundation, your progress toward goals will be unrewarding, unproductive and un-fulfilling.

Today we've examined the first three priorities, Enlightenment, Individualism and Structure. Between now and tomorrow's chapter, I want you to develop specific action steps that you will take to discover more about your priorities.

For Enlightenment, I'd like you to isolate one area you'd like to learn more about and find a book, a cassette series or a class that you will read, listen to or attend so you can get information on a subject you're interested in.

For Individualism, I want you to find a magazine article or a book about a successful person who exemplifies Individualism. Find out how the high priority they gave to Individualism contributed to their success. Almost any issue of "Success" magazine will profile an ideal subject.

For Structure, I'd like you to write down three rules in your life that you've always followed without question. And then try to make up a list of reasons why you should or shouldn't continue following those rules.

This is an important part of the process of the self-examination needed if we are to know ourselves well enough to personalize our step up to success.

# DAY 4

# The Second
# Three Priorities

When we left each other yesterday, I had given you three assignments dealing with the first three priorities we talked about: Enlightenment, Individualism and Structure.

The results of the assignments are very personal, but let's take a couple minutes and review what you were asked to do — and if you had some trouble with the exercise, maybe this can help.

The first assignment related to the Enlightenment priority. As you remember, I told you that no one priority was any better or any worse than any other but it is important that we have at least some strength in each of the six areas if we're going to be successful.

To increase the value you place on Enlightenment, I asked you to isolate one area you'd like to learn more about and find a book or a cassette that will give you information. Maybe you could find a seminar you would like to attend.

So, how did you do? Was it difficult to think of something you really wanted to know more about? What did you pick — a subject that had to do with making money or did you want to find out how to start a business at home? Perhaps you wanted to learn more about how the environment is affected by us and what the rain forest controversy is all about. Was there a hobby you've always wanted to take up but never had the time?

Maybe you decided to finally refresh your understanding of how the government works so you got out your kid's Civics textbook. Not many of us remember all that stuff we were taught in high school. Or did you resolve to learn a new language so you could travel to a country you've always wanted to see and be able to talk to the natives when you get there?

Any answer you came up with that would teach you something you don't know is the correct answer.  The trick is, now that you have made the choice, commit to it.

Don't sit back and say: "I'd really like to know a little bit about physics and what the black hole theory is all about" — and then never do anything about it.  Try reading "A Brief History of Time" or "Black Holes and Baby Universes" by Dr. Stephen Hawking, the brilliant English physicist who is the world expert on black holes and writes about them in language we can understand.  Check with your local colleges and see if they are offering any adult courses in astronomy and physics.

Look through the scientific magazines for interesting articles in laymen's terms.  Remember what we said yesterday: Study anything for half an hour a day, every day for five years and you can be an expert in that subject.  And I'm willing to bet that after you've studied a subject for a little while, you'll find that even if learning just for the fun of learning isn't your top priority,  it will be invigorating and liberating.

The second assignment I gave you was to strengthen your Individualism.  I asked you to find an article or a book about a successful person who exemplifies the value of independence.  Almost any article or book about an inventor or an artist or an entrepreneur would serve the purpose.

The impressionist painters, like Degas and Monet, horrified the art world at the turn of the century because they broke with tradition.  They threw out the concept that paintings had to be classic in subject matter, dark in color and heavy with oil pigments.  Instead, they painted flowers and ballerinas in pastel colors with soft edges.  Their contemporaries were outraged when they broke the mold and set a whole new style.

Inventors, by their very nature, place a high value on Individualism.  They want their world to change so they invent new ways to accomplish old tasks.  They break the rules and make build new roads to old places. Read the life of Thomas Edison or Leonardo DaVinci.  Read Lee Iacocca's book about turning the Chrysler corporation around.  They all broke the rules.

But don't forget that you can go overboard with Individualism.  The rebel genius is a compelling character, but the jails are full of white collar criminals who thought they were above the laws. The bankruptcy courts are kept busy with entrepreneurs who failed because they didn't ask anyone for help. They thought they could reinvent the wheel and they lost everything in the attempt. You need to temper your Individualism with some sense of Structure.

The Structure assignment was a little bit different. I asked you to write down three rules in your life that you followed without question — and then decide whether or not you should continue to follow them.

Obviously, I didn't mean by this that you brush your teeth after meals and yes, you should continue to do so for optimum dental health. That's too simple.

I'm talking more about those rules that everyone has but no one knows exactly where they originated.

Let's say that it has always been an unspoken rule in your family that you get together for Thanksgiving at your parents' house every year. It doesn't matter if you're invited somewhere else or you want to take a vacation for a those four days or you've been given tickets to your college's football game out of town. You have to have Thanksgiving with the family. You can't even consider doing anything else. Now, there's a rule you can consider breaking.

I know someone who lives about a three hour drive from his family. He's a successful entrepreneur and a bachelor who owns his own house and enjoys staying in it. Now, he's in his early fifties and he still goes home for every major holiday with his Mom and his brothers' families. He complains that he'd like them to visit him instead this year and decides that he'll stay at his house — but by the day before the holiday, he's in his car, annoyed and unhappy but dutifully on his way home.

It shouldn't surprise you to know is that this man is also one of the most structured people you'll ever meet. He lives by the rules. His house is immaculate. He doesn't even have a junk drawer. All he has is a lot of stress because he's so often doing things he doesn't want to do.

I want you to break out of some of those old patterns of living. Do things differently this year. Reassess and re-evaluate your life and make sure that you're not letting childhood rules control your adult life. The kids say: "Go with the flow." Well, I want you to make the walls of your Structure priority a little more flexible so you can go with your own flow for a change, instead of someone else's.

Now let's move on to the next three core Priorities that affect how we live our lives — and those are Power, Altruism and Economics.

People who want to control others and who crave influence and importance are people who place a high value on Power.

Politicians would certainly fall into this category, as would officers in the military, judges, royalty and certainly, corporate executives. These are men and women who are happiest when they are controlling everyone around them. They want people to jump when they give a command and to follow their orders without argument. They are usually very self-controlled, too. They can follow a diet without giving in to temptation, they exercise regularly and their clothes are always clean and pressed. They're happiest when they're center stage and in charge.

First-born children in a family are supposed to place a high priority on Power because they're used to being the oldest and being in charge of their younger brothers and sisters.

If you place high value on Power, you want to build vast empires with huge staffs. You enjoy the role of manager. Many successful entrepreneurs fall into this category. These entrepreneurs differ greatly from those who have Individualism as their highest priority.

The Power entrepreneur starts a little company in the garage and builds it into a multi-million dollar business, employing thousands of people. Mary Kay Ash, who founded the Mary Kay Cosmetics company, did this. So did Henry Ford. Rich DeVos and Jay Van Andel took the Amway Corporation from its beginnings in a shed in their backyard to an internationally known corporation. Let's not forget Ray Kroc, who blazed a trail with McDonald's! And, there are a host of other top business people I could name.

On the other hand, the entrepreneur who places more emphasis on Individualism than Power is perfectly happy in a one-person office in the back bedroom at home. If that small office suddenly needs to grow and become a large corporation, the Individualistic entrepreneur will usually sell out and start another project in the home office.

Power people seek the limelight and recognition. Ted Turner, the founder of CNN Cable Television is a good example of this. He loves the pomp and circumstance of Power and, married to Jane Fonda, he enjoys even greater visibility. I've read that the sign on his desk says: "Lead, follow or get out of *my* way!"

High Power individuals are interesting to watch in a corporate setting. They actively seek recognition. Give them a promotion or a bigger office or a better title and they're happy. Add two people to their staff and it's almost better than a raise. Money is not as important to them as prestige.

The same is true in the entertainment world. There are stars who will take less money for higher billing. Their name on the screen means more to them than their bank account.

These people have healthy egos and like to be in the center of the action. They are assertive about their needs and aggressive about fulfilling them. They are more than willing to play all the games necessary to get where they're going and will maneuver to get the recognition they feel they deserve. If you want them on your team, you'd better make them the Captain!

On the other hand, the person who places a low value on Power could be called "the worker bee."

They almost refuse to take credit for their accomplishments. They have no particular interest in climbing the corporate or the social ladder. If they receive recognition, they pass the glory on to their staff. If they are praised for an accomplishment, they're the first to say "I couldn't have done it alone."

They tend to echo General Sherman, who told the Republican National Convention in 1884: "I will not accept if nominated and will not serve if elected." Power was not that important to him.

Prince Charles of England might fall into this category. He seems to me to be very uncomfortable with the thought of being King.

Believe me, I'm not putting down people who have a high Power priority. George Bernard Shaw said: "Power doesn't corrupt men; fools, however, if they get into a position of power, corrupt power." Handled well, Power, in and of itself, is a very positive force and it can be used to accomplish meaningful things. The person who can use Power correctly can build invincible teams and instill in others a strong sense of *self*-empowerment.

Power is only dangerous when it's used negatively to stifle growth and creativity and self-esteem — or when it's used unethically to achieve personal gain — or when it's used frivolously with no regard for the real damage it can do.

This is probably a good time to point out that Power is often relative. The great National Football League referee, Jim Tunney, tells about being at a banquet where he was seated at the Speaker's Table.

A waiter came by, carefully placing one pat of butter on each butter plate. When he came to Jim, Tunney asked him to please leave two pats of butter. "I can't," said the waiter. "I only have enough for one pat at each place." Jim is generally a passive kind of guy but this time he pulled out all the stops. "Do you know who I am? I was on television last week refereeing the Super Bowl. I'm being honored here tonight. And I want two pats of butter!" The waiter looked at him for a second and then said: "Do you know who I am? I'm the guy who *controls the butter.*"

Don't think because someone is unknown that they don't have Power.

Before we go on, there are three questions about Power that I want you to think about. Please stop for a moment, and write down your answers in the workbook.

- **Question Number One:** *Can you name three people who have exhibited a high Power priority and used it well?* **They can be well-known names or someone in your own life who "controls the butter."**

- **Question Number Two:** *Can you name three people who have used their Power negatively instead of positively?* **Again, the people you choose can be famous or not.**

- **And, Question Three:** *In what area of your life do* you *have Power and how can you use it better?*

How did you do? Funny, isn't it? When you're asked to name names, it's harder than you thought it would be.

We talked about some people earlier, but let's see if we can come up with others who put a high priority on Power...and use it well.

Among the world leaders, Lech Walesa, the laborer who led Poland out of Russian domination, certainly comes to mind.

I think of the actor, Arnold Schwarzenegger, who's done so much to get children interested in sports and physical fitness. He uses the Power of his popularity to help make a difference.

In Los Angeles, everyone respects the movie actor, Edward James Olmos, who stepped in during the riots in 1992.

Not only did he expose himself to danger by being very visible and defusing a lot of the tension, but then he pitched in to help with the clean-up. If he hadn't been someone instantly recognizable, someone who had put a high priority on the value of being in the spotlight, he probably wouldn't have made the impact he did on his community.

Then, I asked you to think of some people who misused their Power. This is probably easier because we think of the world's great villains. For instance, Adolph Hitler was a man who craved Power and abused it.

Leona Helmsley, the self-crowned hotel queen of New York, found that all her Power couldn't protect her from a jail sentence when she underpaid her taxes. Her treatment of those who worked for her had been so unkind that they did nothing to help her when the chips were down.

Saddam Hussein would certainly make the list of people who abuse their Power — a list that would be a long one, unfortunately, given the history of our human civilization.

Closer to home, you might have come up with a Boss who was a tyrant to work for — or a teacher who delighted in handing out impossibly long homework assignments over Homecoming weekend. I had one of those, didn't you?

Finally, Question Three was: In what area of your life do *you* have Power and how can you use it better?

If you have kids, the answer to that question is pretty obvious. Everyone wants to be the best parent possible.

If you're thinking that there aren't any other areas where you have any Power, think again. You're a consumer, aren't you? You buy groceries and take in your dry cleaning and shop in malls. You order things over the phone — and you may be called and solicited by various salespeople.

In every one of those cases, you have the Power. You're the person who's "controlling the butter."

Any successful store owner will tell you that the customer is king. Any service business operator — these are the people who clean your rugs or shine your shoes or cut your hair — will tell you if the customer isn't satisfied, the business is in trouble. How do you treat these people who depend on you for their livelihood? What do you say or do to make them feel appreciated? Do you treat others as well as you want to be treated?

Our next priority is: Altruism

This priority almost seems like the opposite of Power — just like Individualism might be viewed as the opposite of Structure.

If you place great value on Altruism, you are very concerned with serving others. You have a strong desire to "give back" to a society or an organization or their families.

You are very sincere in your wish to help others, even at your own expense.

People who put a high priority on Altruism want to share what they have. This doesn't mean just writing checks to a favored charity or giving money to a homeless beggar. These people are willing to invest time and energy without any thought of personal gain.

Mother Theresa is the first person I think of. She may be as close to a living saint as we have today. Without any thought of personal profit, she's dedicated her life to helping other people.

Audrey Hepburn was a celebrity who had a high Altruism priority. Despite having all the trappings of wealth and fame, she still spent her time working with starving children around the world through UNICEF — the United Nations International Children's Emergency Fund.

The person with a high degree of Altruism is often described as being ready to "give you the shirt off their back," — someone you can always go to for help.

Please notice, this is not necessarily the opposite of Power because many people use their Power and influence to help the less fortunate. You can have a high score in both those priorities. They aren't mutually exclusive. But, if the Altruism priority is strongest, there is a higher calling to give to others — even before you give to yourself.

Along with that, in the true altruist, there's almost a fear of recognition. They don't want to be honored or praised or set up as a role model. They just want to make their contribution and go on with life. They don't see their generosity as a cause for acclaim. What may seem remarkable to those of us who have a different priority ranking is perfectly normal to them. This is just how they need to live their lives.

I read recently about a man who had donated more than sixty gallons of blood over his lifetime. At one pint per visit, that's almost five hundred visits to the blood bank. It was his habit to stop in once a month and donate a pint of blood and he'd done it for more than fifty years. He couldn't understand what all the fuss was about. He was just "doing his thing." No big deal.

You'll find people with a high Altruism priority working in every not-for-profit organization in the country. They are the retired executives who lend their expertise to start-up companies. . .men and women who agree to be Big Brothers and Big Sisters to young people who are growing up without one of their parents in the home. . .people who send checks every month to support a hungry child in some disadvantaged country. . . and the volunteers who deliver meals to shut-ins or visit nursing homes.

Is there a dark side to this loving and giving way of life? Well, yes, I suppose so. There are people who take care of others and neglect themselves and their own families. It becomes a case of the old adage about the shoemaker's child who has no shoes. Daddy is so busy fixing everyone else's shoes that he lets his own family go barefoot.

The traits of those who place a low value on Altruism are that they subscribe to the notion that "If I'm okay, then you *must* be."

They believe they can only have value to others by taking care of themselves. Their guidebook is "The Art of Selfishness" — not stinginess — selfishness. Concern with the "self." They aren't necessary cheap but they subscribe to the notion of "me, first...me, only."

Okay, I have more questions that I want you to answer in your personal **Just Say Yes!** Workbook.

- **Here's the First Question:** *What do you actively do to demonstrate Altruism?*

- **Question Number Two is:** *Can you name the last three times you gave up something you wanted to have or do to help somebody else achieve their desires?*

- **And the Third Question:** *Why did you do it and how did you feel about it?*

Write down the answers as fully as you can. When you're finished, we'll continue.

All done? Okay, let's review the questions.

The first one was: What do you do to actively demonstrate Altruism? Well, maybe you serve on the board of your local Community Center or you're a Little League Coach or a Den Mother.

Perhaps you work in your church's Soup Kitchen once a month or help in a Common Pantry. Some people shovel the snow for elderly neighbors or volunteer to drive someone to regular therapy treatments. There are any number of ways in which you could demonstrate your concern for the folks around you.

Question Number Two was even more important. I asked if you can name the last three times you gave up something you wanted to have or do in order to help somebody else achieve their desires?

One of the true signs of Altruism is depriving yourself to benefit someone else. If you can name several times that you demonstrated your concern for the community but you can't name three occasions when it cost you — when you felt the pinch psychologically or financially — then you have to question whether it's true Altruism.

If you serve on the board of the United Way because it will help you get a promotion in your company and because you enjoy being looked up to and respected, that's fine but it's not really costing you anything.

On the other hand, giving up your weekend at Club Med to help out at the Special Olympics — without ever telling anyone what you did — is, perhaps, the purest form of Altruism.

Which brings us to the Third Question: Why did you do it and how did you feel about it? Did you do it so you'd be admired or did you do it because you really cared?

There's a big difference. You need to be honest with yourself when you answer. Were your actions based on Altruism or Power?

Are you beginning to see how these priorities all inter-relate? It's that relationship, in all the varying degrees, that makes us do what we do and that creates or hampers our success.

The final core priority that we're going to talk about is maybe the easiest to understand. If you have your highest score in the Economic column, you place the most importance on money and financial return for your efforts.

That certainly doesn't make you unique. With the cost of living rising every year, we all have to be concerned with money. Making it, spending it, saving it and investing it are fairly universal activities.

But if your highest area of concentration is centered around accumulating money, then it's the Economic priority that drives what you do — and determines how far you'll go along with something just for the financial return.

Even though it's gotten a bad rap over the years, all by itself, money is neither good nor bad. Money isn't to blame for criminals anymore than food is to blame for overeaters.

Think of the how different the uses of money are. It can finance corruption or it can build hospitals. The lack of it can drive humans to murder, or it can inspire them to reach new heights. In a relationship, it make for a good and worthwhile family life, or it can be the catalyst for suspicion and divorce.

You can easily spot the person who's centered on the Economic priority. They'll keep score of everything they do — and that score will always be expressed in terms of dollars won or lost. You'll be pretty sure of where they stand financially and, given an opportunity, they'll tell you just how they earned every dollar. They have financial plans and definite earning goals. They aren't going to waste their time, talent, or energy on any project that isn't going to pay off.  Their motto is: "How much is in it for me?"  And no matter how much money they have, they still want more.

I remember hearing a story about J. D. Rockefeller, Sr. — the President of Standard Oil and the man who built the family's vast fortune.  Old J. D. was born in 1839 and lived to be 98, but he still counted every penny.

Towards the end of his life, he found out his family was going to give him an electric car for his birthday so he could get around his estate more easily.

He put a stop to that in a hurry.  He told them, "If you don't mind, I'd rather have the money."

Now, there's a perfect example of the Economic priority in action.

The title of Donald Trump's book, "The Art of the Deal," also sums up this attitude pretty well.  Nothing is quite as stimulating as commissions, deals, and negotiations.  Their calculator is always right at hand and they make value judgments based on how much money the other fellow has.

If you don't place a particularly high priority on Economics, you'll be less materialistic like the person we hear of, every so often, who lived in abject poverty but had hundreds of thousands of dollars in the bank.

The lesser Economic drive is seen in people who seem to  pay little attention to the monetary results of their decisions.  They may even be rather irresponsible when it comes to handling money because it just isn't that important to them.  It almost gets in their way.

Thomas Edison was one of these people.  When Western Union offered him a hundred thousand dollars for one of his inventions, Edison couldn't deal with a figure that large.  He told them: "The money is safer with you.  Just give me six thousand dollars a year for seventeen years."

He was like a lot of creative people have less interest in money than they do in their own projects which is why they have agents — who all have high Economic priorities! It's often only the agent's fixation on money that makes the artist or actor or writer wealthy.

I have four questions for you to answer in your personal **Just Say Yes!** workbook.  These are designed to help you focus on the value you place on the Economic priority.

■ **Question Number One is:**  *Do you have a personal financial plan?  Have you written your Will and planned for your insurance, housing, savings and retirement needs?  And when did you did you last update them?*

■ **The Second Question is:** *If you were offered a raise, would you work harder — or do you feel you already deserve it?*

■ **Question Three:**  *Name three specific things you've done in your life to make more money.*

■ **And the Fourth Question is:** *How do you feel when a "get rich" proposition comes along?*

Write down you're answers.  We'll talk about them a little bit when you get back.

The First Question I asked you was:  Do you have a personal financial plan?  Have you written your Will and planned for your insurance, housing, savings and retirement needs?  And when did you did you last update them?

Now, you may be saying, "Come on, Scott, of course, I do!  My wife and I took care of all that when we were married."

You'd be surprised how many couples do just that.  When they begin their life together, they plan their budgets and save for their dream house and college tuition for the kids.

But the years go by and those financial plans are rarely every looked at again.  We talk about it a lot but we never get around to doing it.

I know a wealthy family where the parents were always talking about The Will — and when they said "The Will" you knew it was printed in capital letters.  The years passed.  The kids grew up and had families of their own and still they heard about The Will.

Finally, the father died and The Will was read.  It consisted of less than a page, leaving everything to his wife and whoever of his as-yet unborn children survived him.  The Will had been dated the year he was married and almost fifty years later, nothing had been changed.  Of course, the mother's will was a carbon copy of her husband's.

Now, it could have been worse.  They could have neglected to write a Will at all — but by not attending to how the funds were going to be distributed, the family turned over a lot of money to the government in taxes — money that could have been protected in trusts for the children and grandchildren.

A lot of us don't like to think about death.  We don't like to plan for old age and illness.  We avoid getting our affairs in order.  But you must do it.  I can't stress this strongly enough.

Work with your attorney and a licensed financial planner.  And be especially careful when choosing a financial planner.  There are a number of charlatans out there who give financial advice when they have no training and no experience.

You can get the basics in place and working — and by "basics" I mean savings plans, trusts, solid investments that will pay off when you need the money instead of today — when you get them in place, the rest of your financial portfolio will take care of itself.

There is no excuse for not having a will.  There is no excuse for not having a financial plan.  There's  no excuse for not having a regular savings plan.  It doesn't matter if it's five or ten bucks a week, you've got to get into the habit of putting at least five or ten dollars aside every month.  We all go about paying everyone else before we pay ourselves and that leads to financial ruin.

You are as important as anyone you owe money to — so put money in your own account as if you were paying one of your charge cards.

Prepare the foundation and then you can build the rest of your life on it with complete peace of mind because you'll know you're on solid ground.

The Second Question I asked was: If you were offered a raise, would you work harder — or do you feel you already deserve it?

This question deals with how you feel about your job and the people you work for, but it also deals with the value you place on your Economics priority.

If a raise means you'll work harder, it's a pretty good sign that money is what motivates you.

Question Three was: What are three specific things you've done in your life to make more money?

If you can't think of any, you probably don't place a high priority on money.

If you did, you'd think of three things you did this month, let alone over a lifetime. You'd be able to list part-time jobs or businesses on the side that you have to make extra income. These aren't hobbies — unless your hobbies bring in cash. If you want to keep yourself motivated in the future, all you have to do is find a way to tie an economic reward on everything you do.

The Fourth and Final Question was: How do you feel when a "get rich" proposition comes along?

There are some people who aren't interested in taking any kind of chance to increase their wealth — and that's a little short-sighted.

Just be sure to review any plan very carefully and discuss it with people who are more knowledgeable than you are.

On the other hand, don't be one of the people who constantly jumps into get rich schemes and usually gets burned. You need to find the balance — and we'll be talking about that just a little later on.

What I want you do be able to do is to strengthen your Economics priority to the point that you're able to objectively analyze financial propositions when they are presented to you. Your analysis and good judgment are going to be big contributors to your financial security in the years ahead.

To conclude this chapter, I'm going to give you an assignment, much like the one I gave you yesterday, based on the three priorities we've discussed.

One, I want you to choose an area of Power that you have and find different ways to exercise it. For instance, you might want to be more dramatic or forceful in your exercise of Power — or you might want to be less intense.

To work on your Altruism priority, I want you to do one good thing for someone in the next twenty-four hours without anyone knowing about it. Do it — and see how you feel about it.

And finally, in terms of Economics, if you haven't gotten your life in order the way we discussed, with your Will and your financial plan firmly in place, I want you to get the basic process started during the next twenty-four hours.

And while you're at it, make a list of what new set of dreams and opportunities would come along if you had money.  Make a list. Figure out how you'd balance out your life if you could afford more.

When you have the assignment written into your workbook, join me tomorrow and we'll talk about some of the trade-offs that we have to make between our priorities if we're going to Step Up to Success.

**DAY 5**

# Priorities:
# Balance & Trade-Offs

Before we left each other yesterday, I gave you three assignments about the priorities of Power, Altruism and Economics. I hope you took the time to write out the answers in your personal workbook. I can't stress this too much. It is only by participating fully this self-discovery process that you will learn how to **Just Say Yes!** and Step Up to Success.

The first assignment I gave you was to choose an area of personal Power in your life and find different ways to exercise it. I suggested that you might want to be more dramatic or forceful — or you might want to be less intense in demonstrating your control.

As is often true in these exercises, your answers are neither right nor wrong. They are intensely personal and the only score you get is a feeling that you know yourself a little bit better and can handle your life with more confidence and clarity.

I would like to know which Power situation in your life you chose. Are you in a position at your work where you have people reporting to you? How do they think about you? Even better, how would you like to work for *you*? (Professional speaker Ed Foreman says many people have assured him they would quit before they would do that!)

Studies have shown that workers respond more to praise than they do to money or time off. People want to know their efforts have been noticed. Think what you can you do tomorrow to express your appreciation to your team.

I know one Boss who used to call his department together four or five times a year for an impromptu ice cream party in the middle of the afternoon. The staff got a chance to sit together for half an hour and unwind as friends and colleagues. Even though it wasn't planned that way, a lot of business was discussed and the department morale was high.  It was an easy and inexpensive way to say "thank you for a job well done."

If your personal Power center is in the home, have you found a way to teach your children what you expect of them without yelling?  Do you spend as much time telling them what they have done *right* as you do telling them what they've done wrong?

Are you spending quality fun time with your family instead of always complaining about how much work you have to do?  How often do you say "I love you — no matter what you do!"?  Did you think of some ways to change how you interact with those around you?

The second priority we talked about was Altruism, and the assignment I gave you was to do one good thing for someone without anyone knowing about it — and then see how you feel about it.

Your choices on this one are almost endless.  You could have sent flowers to a friend who's having a tough time and enclosed a card that only said:  "I know you're hurting and I care."

Leo Buscaglia tells the story of driving home after his father's funeral, grieving and very much alone.  As he dragged himself up the stairs to his front door, he found a bouquet of flowers and a chocolate cake waiting for him — with no idea who had left them.  As he tells the story, no flowers ever smelled sweeter and no dessert every tasted better.  It was a gift of love that required nothing of him — not even a thank you.

Whatever you chose to do anonymously, how did you feel afterwards?  I'll bet you felt better than you did before.  In giving of yourself, you received an even greater reward.

And finally, to strengthen your Economics priority, I urged you to take the necessary steps to ensure your financial affairs are in order.  Is your Will up-to-date?  Are your children provided for in case something happens to you?

Have you appointed guardians for them and protected any money you leave them?  You may think you don't have any money to worry about, but if you die in an accident, there may be millions in insurance settlements.

Your family deserves to be planned for.

If you need to do work on this phase of your life, you should have made an appointment with your lawyer and a financial advisor so you can be confident about your future. If you didn't do it last night, it should be on the top of today's agenda.

I also asked you to list a new set of dreams and opportunities that would come along if you didn't need to worry about money. I want you to realize the difference that learning to **Just Say Yes!** is going to make in your life. These aren't the improbable dreams we dreamt on Day One where you had all the money you could ever spend.

No, these are the dreams we all have for things like a vacation home or maybe a nifty little sports car that's all yours — no sharing with your spouse or teenagers — or a cruise to some exotic place — or an addition to the house.

What were your dreams? How do you plan to fulfill them? We're going to start working on that as we begin talking about the balance and trade-offs that are essential if we're going to make our priorities work for us.

As we've discussed the six basic priorities, I'm sure you've gotten a better idea of how much value you put on each one and how each affects your behavior.

You see, every one of us has each of the priorities in our value structure but in varying amounts. I rank them differently than you do — and you rank them differently than the person next to you. This is part of what might be called our psychological DNA — that part of us that makes us absolutely distinct from anyone else.

If you refer back to the test you took at the end of Day Two, you'll see how you scored in each of the priority categories. Remember the order in which you ranked them. Each priority, from number six to number one, is a step you'll use to reach success.

As you look at the order of your priorities, I want you to be very certain that your ranking reflects how *you* feel and not the choices someone else has made for you. The Army used to be famous for this. A young man would be drafted and it would be known that he was a highly qualified mechanic with a fear of heights. So where did the Army put him — not in the Motor Pool, you can be sure of that. No, they would send him for paratrooper training.

Well, life is a little like that — only we don't have to follow orders. I told you about the guidance counselor who decided I was going to stay home, live on the farm, and work in the store the rest of my life. If he'd had his way, that's all I'd ever have been trained for.

His reality would have become mine, whether I liked it or not.

What has happened to you? In your personal relationships, did you let your parents dictate the career you were going to study for in college?

I know of a guy whose father was a skilled woodworker. Examples of his talent can still be seen in scores of buildings in San Francisco. But when his only son wanted to work with him and carry on the tradition, the father said "no." The son was sent to college to become an engineer — and today he's a respected professional.

But ask Bob what he would really like to be doing and he'll take you to his workshop and show you the intricate woodworking projects that occupy his spare time. That's where his heart is — however, the decision was taken out of his hands.

I think that's one of life's little tragedies. We only get one time around on this carousel. How sad that we can't spend it doing what we enjoy.

The same sort of thing happens professionally. Let's look at a not uncommon case history. Let's say Marty joins a company as a street salesperson. He enjoys the customer contact. He knows the product inside out. He exceeds his quota every month. Marty works hard and is clearly the star of the department. Life's good. He's doing what he wants.

In due course, Marty is promoted to Sales Manager. He misses the daily customer contact but he's still heavily involved in sales so everything's fine. Then, there's a realignment of departments and all of a sudden, Marty's in the Marketing Department. Now, he's getting removed from his area of expertise — but he's been made a vice-president and the salary is great, so he tries to keep his hand in sales...but, he doesn't have much time for his own interests.

A few more years pass, and Marty's elevated to President of the company. He's got the Power. He's got the perks. And he's got the Economic security. Everything's great, right?

Wrong.

Marty ends up having a heart attack in his early fifties. The doctor said it's stress but, deep down, Marty knows the real truth. He's lived too many years of his life being what other people wanted him to be. He wanted to be a street salesman. The last thing he wanted was to run the company.

Sound far-fetched? Well, it happens every day. Marty isn't so different from the rest of us. How many times have you heard people say: "I'd love to do so-and-so but I can't make a living at it." So, they settle for something else.

There's a brilliant book written by Dr. Marsha Sinatar. The title says it all: *Do What You Love and the Money Will Follow*. The author's message is not only that you don't have to do what you dislike but that you will do much better if you follow your heart.

It's also possible that you have a very different priority than someone who's close to you. If you can't realize and celebrate the differences, your relationship is headed for trouble.

If you care about your priority of Individualism and your spouse is only interested in making money — Economics — you could have a problem, especially if you work together.

I know of a couple who run a very successful company. They've built it from a tiny garage start-up into a multi-million dollar organization. But, when you're with the owners, it's immediately apparent that they're coming from different priorities. He wants to invent new machinery and create new ways to develop product. She, on the other hand, only looks at the bottom line. Everything she says somehow comes back to money.

Imagine how much easier their relationship would be if they could recognize and applaud each other's strengths — instead of fighting for priority dominance. While their love for each other is very apparent, it exists in an atmosphere of constant bickering.

What a non-productive way to live!

It's very possible that you have looked at your mission priority ranking and worked through the exercises the past two days and now you realize that you aren't living in harmony with what you really want.

Perhaps you feel you'd be happiest if you could contribute something to the community on a daily basis but between your work and your family, your schedule doesn't leave you time to volunteer.

So, think about changing your job. Almost every non-profit organization has a paid staff — people who earn their living helping others.

If you rank Altruism and Economics as your two highest priorities, think about fundraising as a career. Not-for-profits are always seeking new sources of income so fund-raisers make money for the organization and themselves while providing a lot of good.

If you're a person whose skill lies in communications, there are arts and societal issues that need to be articulated to the public. If you're an attorney, you can do more pro bono work — which means you take on deserving clients who can't afford to pay.

You get the idea. Just look at your old skills with a fresh eye and you'll see a whole new picture.

Please don't feel that somehow you've failed if your priorities have changed!

Maybe you left college with definite goals you wanted to achieve by your fortieth birthday. When you turned forty and you were close to your goals but found something is missing — you're unsatisfied and you don't know why.

It's probable that your priority has changed over the years. It's likely that you don't like the same music and don't spend your time with the same friends doing the same things that you were passionate about at twenty.

Why shouldn't your priorities change, too? Maybe now you would rather spend time studying than working those twelve-to-fourteen hour days. That's fine. It's normal.

You'll be less frustrated and more fulfilled if you adjust your schedule to fit your priorities. Many colleges and universities boast instructors and professors who spent time in the real world — and then went back to school, where they are happiest, so they can teach what they have learned.

The point is, no matter what you are doing or what you want to do, there *is* a way to accomplish it. The real job is to know yourself well enough to know what you really want. Start planning for your second career while you're still working on your first one.

Recently, I ran across a quote from the brilliant actress, Meryl Streep, in which she said: "Integrate what you believe in every single area of your life. Take your heart to work and ask the most and best of everybody else, too. Don't let your special character and values, the secret that you know and no one else does — *the truth* —

don't let that get swallowed up by the great chewing complacency."

Isn't that great?

"The great chewing complacency" — I like that. It's sort of a modern day phrasing of Henry David Thoreau's often-quoted line from *Walden Pond:* "The mass of men lead lives of quiet desperation."

Whether it's "quiet desperation" or "the great chewing complacency," I think a lot of us are leading our lives that way — and isn't that a sad commentary?

That's what this program is all about — getting out of that rut you've been in so long that it looks like the highway to you.

And to do it, you've got to establish a sense of priority balance.

Have you ever seen a knitter finish part of a sweater and, while it's still on the needles, pull it into shape? This way the yarn is distributed evenly among the stitches and the length and width actually change to accommodate the balancing.

Our lives are like that.

We have to take the time to stop and pull at our priorities until they are in balance.

Say you're one of those entrepreneurial types, like I am, and you work in a highly structured environment. Now, you like your job just fine. It satisfies what you need in terms of Power and Economics. What you don't like is having to obey so many rules. You'd like to spend a little more time developing your mind instead of your bank account.

The way you see it, if you toe-the-line until retirement, then you can do whatever you want — but retirement is sure a long way off.

Wait a minute! You have options here.

You like your job but you want more unstructured time. Check and see if you can work at home one day a week. For many people, a home office makes great good sense and in this era of computers and modems and FAX machines, physical presence in the office isn't always necessary. If your particular job doesn't allow for that kind of flexibility, set aside a space in your home — it can be in the garage or the basement or a spare bedroom — and create your own, personal environment. In this area — and I would suggest you set it off with walls and a door — in this area you are the supreme ruler. You can paint the walls any color you want.

You can make it as messy or neat as you want. You can do anything in that room that you want — even some of the studying that you feel your life lacks. You might not have to spend more than a half hour a day — or a couple of hours a week — there. What you will have given yourself is permission to follow no one's rules but yours — at least one place in your life.

It's interesting that once you have that permission, you may find you don't need to exercise it all that often. Lots of times we want what we can't have — and then when our prayers are answered, the urgency and upset are greatly diminished.

The other priority you had in this hypothetical situation was the need to learn more, to spend more time with non-professional pursuits.

Again, talk to your company. It's possible that they will pay for you to take college courses that are connected with your job. If not, go to your local college and check out their adult education schedules. If you live in a fairly urban area, you'll find organizations that offer two and three session courses on any number of subjects, taught by people who actually work in the field. It's a great way to learn a new skill.

If all else fails, go spend one night a week at your local library — or spend your lunch hour there every few days instead of eating out. It'll help satisfy the need to stimulate your intellect.

At my seminars, audience members invariably come up with a lot of solutions to life's dissatisfactions. As a group, it's easy for them to see how our lives can be adjusted to fit in all the areas of interest a person needs. It just proves the strength of the group dynamic. When individual participants were working on their challenges alone at home, they seemed insurmountable.

The reason for this is very simple.

At home, you set up your own negative cheering section. In the seminar setting, with several minds focused on the challenge, the answers fall into place.

We've all heard Napoleon Hill's line from *Think and Grow Rich* about being able to achieve anything you can imagine and believe in strongly enough.

I contend that may not be exactly true.

I know that as much as I'd like to play center for the Lakers, at my age, in my physical condition, and not even six feet tall (with a seven inch vertical leap!), I'm not going to make it — I don't care how much I want to.

But, that's not really the point.

If I want to play basketball — I can do that. I can find a group of people who also had dreams of the pros and couldn't cut it — and we can have just as much fun playing the game — if that's what I really want.

If it's the Power and Economics of being an NBA center that interests me most, then I have to find another career option that will provide them.

There again, I have to decide what is most important to me. I can't make everything my number one priority. You'd carry me out on a stretcher after the first month. There's no way to serve that many masters. As we said before, while every priority has its positive aspects, only the top ones on your list deserve the bulk of your concentrated time and effort.

This is where trade-offs come into the picture. There are priorities you have that will have to be put in the background for awhile so you can concentrate on other priorities that are more dominant.

For instance, say your number one priority is Individualism. You really need to run your own show. You like to be alone and answer to no one.

That's fine. However, before you can do that, you have to have a skill or experience that is marketable. Very few consultants are right out of college. Experience is necessary so that you have something to sell that's worth the money you need to be paid.

The same is true if you're a writer. It's the unusual author who's in their twenties when they become famous. It takes time to have enough life experience to write about. Many writers will say they didn't start writing until they were in their forties or fifties or sixties because they just didn't have enough to say before then. They hadn't seen and done enough yet. In the meantime, they work at other jobs while gaining the experience and insight they need.

So, if your priority is being an independent contractor, and entrepreneur, you may have to make the trade-off of working in a structured environment for a few years until you learn your business or your craft well enough to have someone pay for your services.

To make the waiting time more palatable for yourself, try putting a multi-year calendar up on the wall where you can see it every day and then circle the date you plan to quit your job and go out on your own.  Nobody else needs to know what that circle means but it will be a constant reminder to you of where you're going and when.

We'll start talking about goals tomorrow and you'll learn more about how to give yourself a specific focal point to aim at so that your present becomes a rosy path to the future — instead of a bed of hot coals.

During the time you have to spend trading off one priority for another, you can try several different avenues.  You may find that what looked like your number one priority really isn't when you've had an opportunity to spend some time exploring it.

This is when you solidify your choices.

This is the time when you identify the mission priority that you will devote the most energy to and then zero in on it with laser intensity.  Make very sure that this is what you want to be doing in the next few years.

And, never forget, there's no shame in changing your mind. Remember Jerry Rubin, one of the most prominent radicals in the Sixties?  With Tom Hayden and others, he was one of the most militant of the Chicago Seven.  His every waking breath seemed to be dedicated to social reform — and whether or not you approve of the methods he used, he was successful.  That was the young Jerry Rubin who hated capitalism and all it stood for.  Today, Jerry Rubin is a millionaire many times over as an executive in a multi-level marketing company.  His Altruism priority has been lessened and his Economics value has come on strong.

Tom Hayden is another former rebel who has mainstreamed into business and politics.  And that's all right!

No one should have to live forever with the choices they made when they were many years younger.

By the same token, there are examples of people who have changed their lives in other directions — like the corporate executive who gave it all up to become a contemplative monk — or Harry Truman, the haberdashery salesman who became President of the United States.

One of the important considerations of the trade-off

arrangement is that you are always going to have to give up something.

It's like the basic negotiating principle that says you should never sit down at the bargaining table if you're not willing to walk away when the deal isn't right.

You're going to have to realize that there will be times you miss your son's soccer game because you're attending to a higher priority — for example, attending a conference out-of town that will help you earn money for his college education.

I know the president of a company that is centered on learning for children. He is a dedicated professional who spends long hours bringing the company's uplifting message to parents. His own children, however, hardly see him. He has had to trade-off one priority for another.

Mr. Rogers, of children's television fame, is another parent who has been accused of being an absentee father — while being the only father many young viewers ever knew.

Again, I'm *not* saying this is right or wrong — I'm just saying each of us has to make our own choice and realize that for every positive there may be a negative trade-off.

There's another trait I want you to work on during these two weeks of self-analysis and preparation for the time when you **Just Say Yes!** — and that trait is concentration. You need to focus clearly and without distraction on the future you have planned for yourself.

Thomas Edison was asked what he felt was the primary contributor for success in any field and he said: "The ability to apply your physical and mental energies to one problem incessantly without growing weary."

The English writer, Thomas Carlyle, wrote: "The weakest living creature, by concentrating his powers on a single object, can accomplish something; whereas the strongest, by dispersing his over many, may fail to accomplish anything."

And, Alexander Graham Bell may have inadvertently revealed the process by which he invented the telephone when he said: "Concentrate all your thoughts upon the work at hand. The sun's rays do not burn until brought to a focus."

If you're constantly starting projects and then leaving them unfinished while you go off to do something else — if you consistently put-off the ground work you know you have to do so you can spend another night in front of television or snoring on the couch — if you reject the opportunity to grow for the future so that you can enjoy the present for a while...

...it's fine!

That's right — *I said it's fine* — but you should put your goals aside and put your dreams away because without single-minded concentration, you don't stand much chance of realizing them.

What happens is the focus, the concentration, the single thinking that we bring to the future we're building is what generates the momentum we have to have if we're going to succeed. We have to have a starting place and we have to have markers along the way.

You also have to have an end point in sight...but don't be surprised if you veer to the right or the left of that end point when the time comes — or you might blast right on through it to an even higher end that takes you farther than you ever dared dream.

Between today and tomorrow, I want you to think about your trade-offs and priorities. Take a couple of pages in your workbook.

At the top of one page, write Priorities. At the top of the other page, write Trade-Offs.

Now, list your priorities in the order of their importance. Don't just put down general categories, like Altruism or Enrichment. Again, I want you to be very specific.

You want to volunteer for the Special Olympics. You want to back to school and get your M.B.A. You want to put a swimming pool in the backyard. You want to have money in the bank — and put down the exact amount you want. All this goes under your Priorities.

On the page under Trade-Offs, I want you to write down what you're willing to give up to achieve your priorities. If you're going to have a pool, it means saving your family vacation money for however many years. So, you find fun things to do in your own area for a couple of summers so you can achieve your goal. Again, don't be vague. Be very definite about where you want your life to be and what you're willing to do to get there.

# DAY 6

# Setting Your Goals, Part One

Yesterday, which was Day Five of our "Just Say Yes! A Step Up to Success" Program, I gave you the assignment of writing down your Priorities and Trade-Offs. You listed your Priorities in order of their importance. I hope you were very specific about these. I want your list to contain actual events you want to have happen in your life.

Maybe you want to start a family within a year. You want to add a room to the house as a play space for the baby. You want to visit relatives you've never met who live in another country. You want to have plastic surgery. Whatever it is, no matter how serious or trivial it may appear to others, these are *your* priorities, in whatever order of importance they fall.

After you got your Priority List together, I asked you to take another piece of paper and write the heading: Trade-Offs. On this sheet, I wanted you to list the things you'd have to give up to accomplish your priority list.

You might even have to give up — or put off — a priority.

For instance, you may not be able to have the plastic surgery if you want to build an addition on the house. The trip abroad may have to wait until the baby bills are paid. You and your spouse may each have to work two jobs for a few months to get far enough ahead so you can afford to live on one salary for a period of time before and after the baby is born.

It boils down to one of the basic laws of physics: For every action, there is an equal and opposite reaction. For everything you want, there is something you have to give up. It is the very rare person who gets to have it all.

I want you to keep the lists you made very close to you while we talk about goals today and tomorrow. It's vital that you know exactly what your Priorities and Trade-Offs are in front of you as you plan the activities that will take you where you want to go in life.

You'll find at the end of these fourteen days, that each of these assignments is like a separate piece of a jigsaw puzzle.

While individually they may not make much sense, when you look at them together, you'll find they make a new and exciting picture of what your future can hold.

Now, let's turn to today's topic. What do you think about when you hear the word "goals?"

I'm willing to bet that if you're like most people, you don't think about very much. We hear so much about setting and achieving goals that we tune out. Goals become like exercise and diets — something we seriously plan to start working on tomorrow. We become like Scarlett O'Hara: "Tomorrow is another day." We can fix anything in the morning. What harm can another twenty-four hours do?

There are varying statistics as to how many people actually have set goals for their lives. Some studies say as high as ten percent, others say as low as one percent of all people have solid, written goals they are working towards.

As I travel around, whenever people tell me that they have goals, I stop to talk to them about them.

I want to know what the goals are and why they were set and how they're going to be attained and when it may happen. As we talk, we usually find out that they aren't really talking about goals. They're describing wishes or dreams or ideas, but they're not describing goals. And that's really amazing. Somehow we can never seem to define our goals but we are able to make other plans that are very specific.

For instance, if I ask you what you plan to do for your vacation this year, you'll probably have a pretty good idea. You'll have it all planned out. You'll tell me: "As soon as the kids get out of school, we're going to pile in the car and drive to Orlando so we can see Disney World. We'll spend three days at Magic Kingdom and two days at Epcot Center. One afternoon we'll go see Shamu, the Killer Whale. Then, we're going to drive home and see Rock City. We're also going to spend a couple days with the grandparents on our way through Atlanta." You can tell me with great precision where you're going and what you're doing on your vacation. You can most likely even describe the luggage you're going to pack and the clothes you're going to take with you and how much it's going to cost.

Then, my next question is: "Where are you going to be at work or professionally this time a year from now?"

The response I hear to that is quite different. "What? Have you heard a rumor? Is the company in some kind of trouble? Should I be worrying?"

What does this tell you? It simply means that people plan their vacations with more attention and foresight than they plan their lives. They take control of two weeks out of every fifty-two. The rest of the time they let their company or their family move them along like lemmings to the edge of the cliff.

They're like a human herd, moving placidly where they're led — maybe even stampeding occasionally — but never getting anywhere because they don't know where they're going. Kind of frightening, isn't it?

Why does this happen? I think it's because your vacation only comes once a year. If you mess it up, you won't have another chance until next year. You look forward to those two weeks for months and you don't take any chances that might spoil your fun.

But, when it comes to where your life is going to be a year from now, you don't tend to plan quite as well. Maybe it's because you feel you have control over your vacation but you can't help what happens to you in life. Well, I would hope we've dispelled that idea by now but if we haven't, you can be sure it will be gone by the time you've worked through the **Just Say Yes!** process.

The other thing that I find is most of us are very good at making excuses for not having goals.

"I don't need to have goals because I know where I'm going." "I don't need to spend time writing out a lot of goals because things never work out for me." "I'm on the right track — all I have to do is work hard and keep my nose clean and I'll be fine."

In my personal experience, I'd estimate that about one percent of the people I deal with have rock-solid goals. That means ninety-nine out of one hundred people I meet and work with don't have the kind of goals that we're going to be talking about in this session.

And, that has held true over two decades of speaking around the world.

What makes it most interesting is that statistics show only about one percent of people actually get what they really, really want in life. One percent have goals and one percent get what they want — would you say there's a pattern emerging here?

If only one percent have goals and only one percent are truly achieving and getting what they want in life, I don't think it's any coincidence that goal-directed people who have set goals based upon their value priorities are the folks who are finding the pot of gold at the end of their personal rainbows.

Any time we get on this subject, one of the challenges is that too many speakers and self-help writers and self-development trainers talk about goals and their audiences are burned out. In other words, speakers get down on one knee, rip out our chest hairs, swing from the chandelier, pull up the turf, tear down the end posts and yell that you've got to have goals — and we do it so often — that it's become a turn-off.

Speakers have become so evangelistic that many people roll their eyes when we mention "goals" — and that's too bad because what we're not examining what goals are in the *true* sense.

During the next few days, I'm going to make some suggestions to you about what goals are — suggestions that might be a little different from what you've heard before. We're going to add a different spin, a different slant — a different twist on what goals are so we can make them more effective for you.

Two  points as we get started here.  First — and I've said this before and will probably say it again before we're through — *Do It!* Go through this process!  You are establishing for yourself your own individual, unique, personal system for success. Allow yourself to go through the process. Don't short circuit yourself at this point.

Number Two,  it's never too early and it's never too late to establish goals for your life. A friend of mine, very early, established as his goal to be president of a company by the time he was thirty years old.

Now, I've got to admit, as much as I talk and get excited about personal achievement and goal setting, there was a side of me that said: "Well, sure, Tim, good luck and all that. . . "

Well, surprise on me! He didn't realize his goal at thirty — he made it by *twenty-eight!* He's president of the second largest manufacturer of school buses in the world. He's an amazing young man and he's doing wonderful things, but it didn't just happen. It's because of his single-focus goal direction.

The 1956 Olympic Gold Medal winner in the Decathlon was Milt Campbell. He set individual records that haven't been broken to this day. When Milt was a skinny little twelve-year-old kid in New Jersey, he set a goal. He was going to be the Greatest Athlete in the World. Those were the words he used. He wrote them down. He repeated them to himself — and to anyone who would listen — day after day. And, he worked on his skills.

At eighteen, in 1952, he made the team and won the Silver Medal in the Decathlon, the most grueling of all Olympic events.

Four years later, having graduated from Indiana University, he beat out Rafer Johnson and won the Gold Medal. When the newspapers covered the story, one headline read: "Milt Campbell: The Greatest Athlete in the World."

He'd reached his goal.

Today, Milt is a professional speaker who works with corporate audiences and youth groups, instilling the secret techniques that won him the Gold. He is living proof that you can set a goal at twelve and make it come true.

It's never too early to set goals for yourself and what you want to do and where you're going, but it's never too late, either. I told you that Colonel Sanders started KFC with his first Social Security check. Grandma Moses, the world-renowned painter of American primitives, didn't start painting until she was retired. In his book, *Being the Best*, Denis Waitley tells of a neighbor who planted orange and grapefruit seedlings in his backyard when he was in his early eighties, even though it would take at least four years before they bore fruit.

He wasn't going to let age deter him from his goal. And it didn't. He lived to watch his trees flower and bear delicious fruit.

There are numerous stories about marathon runners who never got off the couch until they were in their fifties. There are millionaires who rose from bankruptcy to wealth in their mid-life. Men and women who have returned to college — or even high school — after their children were grown. I saw someone in the paper a few years ago who graduated from college alongside her granddaughter! You know these are all people with firm goals.

So, it's never too early and it's never too late. Wherever you are on the pathway, going through this process will move you towards the enriching life we all want.

Another thing I want you to remember is that goals aren't set in stone. They aren't carved in granite. You can change and adapt your goals as you move towards them. There's the old proverb everyone's mother said at one time or another: "Be very careful what you want — you just might get it."

The point is that too often we set our sights on one thing we want more than anything else in the world — and then one day it's there — and we don't care anymore.

I think of a friend who always wanted a Corvette — specifically, a red Corvette. He dreamed about it. He had pictures of it on his mirror. When he could, he'd stop in at the dealer and take a test drive. It became the obsession of his life but there was always some reason he couldn't realize his goal. He married young and then there were the children's braces and college tuitions. The house needed remodeling — you know how it goes. But, my friend's goal remained unchanged. Finally, in his fifties, he bought his red Corvette. His lifetime goal sat in his driveway.

However, there was a problem.

At his age, he wasn't really comfortable in a sports car without the comforts of a larger vehicle. The goal had been attained but he'd forgotten that he wasn't the same person he was when he'd first set his sights on the car of his dreams. He hadn't stopped to re-evaluate, and therefore the reward wasn't all that satisfying. Within a year, he traded in the Corvette on a luxury sedan.

In this **Just Say Yes!** Process, you'll learn to re-assess your goals regularly so you don't waste time trying for a sports car when you really want a station wagon!

What is *your* ultimate goal? If your ultimate goal is what makes you ultimately successful and ultimately enriched in life, when did Ronald Reagan set his ultimate goal to become President of the United States?

Let's say Mr. Reagan set a goal to be President of the United States early in his life. If he did, then going to Des Moines to be a radio announcer and then to Hollywood to be an actor wouldn't seem to be the normal pathway you'd take to White House.  No, Ronald Reagan's ultimate goal evolved along the way as he was achieving other goals.  It exposed him to new opportunities.

Don't think that you have to set ultimate goals today.  The main thing is to build your momentum through the goal-setting process.

As you start to set your goals, you need to understand the five criteria that every goal must meet if it is to be different from simple hopes, wishes and dreams.   It's these five criteria that make your goal-setting really work.

Without them, your goals won't work.  You won't be motivated to reach them.  If each goal doesn't meet these criteria, it's like trying to build a house without a blueprint or tools.  It's a nice dream but it will never become a reality.

Today, we're going to study the first two criteria and we'll talk about the remaining three tomorrow.

The first criterion of any valid goal is that it be *specific.*

The more specific you can make a goal...the more precise you can make it..then the greater the likelihood that you will achieve it.

By specific, I mean that you don't just set a goal of buying a new, state-of-the-art stereo system.  Instead, you do your homework.  Visit the electronics stores.  Listen to the various equipment that's available.  Plan out the system you want, with brand names and model numbers for each component.  Visualize exactly where it will sit in your home.  Will the cabinets be black or silver?  Where will the speakers be installed?  Will you pay for it on time or wait until you have the cash?  How much can you afford to save each month?  How long are you willing to spend paying it off?  What will the difference be in cost between a cash and a credit purchase?

Be specific to the last detail.  Then — and only then — will you have a valid goal.

On the other hand, if you simply say: "I want my tapes and CD's to sound better,"  then you are doing nothing more than wishing.

It's like a child wishing to be a Ninja Turtle.  It's only make-believe.  You aren't doing anything to move yourself closer to what you want.

I've always liked the story of the concert pianist who was approached by a fan after a concert.  The fan was effusive with her praise and said:  "I would give anything to play like you."  The pianist smiled and said: "If that were true, you *would* play like I do."

So often we say we'd give anything to have something or be something or do something, but when push comes to shove, we don't do anything more than wish. We want the end result, but we never stop to think of the specific steps along the way that need to be taken.

It's cruel irony that the saddest people are those who say: "My only goal in life is to be happy. If I could just be happy for a little while." The irony is that the people who say that probably won't ever be happy.

Why? Because happiness, in itself, isn't specific enough to be an achievable goal.

Happiness is the by-product you get in the progressive achievement toward a priority-oriented goal.

If you want to be happy, you have to set a goal that relates to your dominant priority — then you have to put out some effort to achieve it by utilizing the workable system we're developing.

One of the things I ask people who have non-specific goals is: "If your goal is to be happy, how will you know when you've achieved it?" The answers I get are usually something like: "I can't put it into words. I'll just know it when I'm happy."

Then I ask, "What's it going to take to make you happy?" What I usually hear back is: "I don't know. If I knew, I'd be doing it." If you recognize yourself in that example, I hate to tell you but you'll never find the happiness you're looking for.

Happiness comes from the achievement of specific goals. Happiness isn't a goal in itself — it's a by-product. A friend has a sign in her office that says: "Happiness isn't having what you want. It's wanting what you have." Too many times, we go looking for happiness as an end in itself — and all we'll ever attain is frustration.

You'll find that as you go through this process you'll need to continually refine, close in and narrow your goal, making it more precise and more specific. You have to feel it and see it, you've got to taste it and touch it. You have to know what your life will be like after you've achieved it. You have to have a time-line so you know when you can expect to have it realized.

You've got to have such a specific, detailed vision of what you want to have happen that you're able to visualize it completely and precisely.

The first of the five criteria of successful goals is that they have to be specific.

The second criterion is that goals must be *realistic.*

That's something we don't usually hear speakers talking about, right? We don't read about realism enough in personal development books.

We touched upon this earlier. Remember, I told you yesterday that I'd love to be the center for the Los Angeles Lakers? It would be a totally unrealistic goal for me and one that wouldn't motivate me to achieve.

Now, many self-help "gurus" will tell you that: "You can be anything you want to be — if you want to be it badly enough."

Okay, that's great. If I can't be a pro basketball player, my second choice is: Pope!

What a great job! No one ever tells you you're wrong. You have a lot of power and prestige. You do a lot of good for other people, have plenty of time to study and meditate and no money worries. It's a dream career. I can conceive it and believe it but can I achieve it? I don't think so.

In the history of the Catholic Church, the Cardinals have never chosen a married, American Methodist for the job!

You and I both know I'm never going to be Pope. It might be a nice daydream but it will never happen. It's not realistic.

Goals should make us stretch but they shouldn't be so impossible that they discourage us.

What I want you to do is examine your situation and set goals that make sense in the framework of your life and priorities. In other words, set goals for realistic achievement. Don't set goals that will defeat you because they're so impractical.

What I've found is that most of us don't set unrealistic goals. We set unrealistic time-frames. We have become a society of fast food dinners and microwave ovens and instant achievement. We want it and we want it now. We don't want to wait for anything.

One of my favorite posters shows two vultures sitting on a tree branch. The headline is: "Give me patience God, but hurry." We all have a little of that in us.

That's the promise that many of the infomercials offer: "Get rich quick. We're going to make you rich right away. Use this product and you'll be more in shape, prettier, thinner, or more intelligent overnight." Unfortunately, usually the only people who are getting rich are the people who are selling the program — and they're already in shape, pretty, thin, and intelligent.

See, what we're talking about here is a way to enrich your life and make it last — a way to enrich your existence and make that enrichment continue for the rest of your life. We're not talking about a *quick* fix — but we are talking about a fix.

We're talking about true success within a realistic time-frame.

Think about how life has changed for the faster. Don't you get annoyed when you're driving through a drive-through at McDonald's and they tell you you'll have to pull up and wait for a minute?

I know I get frustrated. I want that Big Mac...and I want it now!

As a society, we don't want to wait for anything. We need to FAX letters instead of putting them in the mail — "FAX it to me! I need it now. I don't want to have to wait." Federal Express has become an enormously successful company because we have to have the package absolutely, positively tomorrow morning — not two days from now, tomorrow!

If you're like me, when you order software for your computer from the catalog, you always opt for the next day delivery. I've functioned without this program for your entire life but now I have to have it within twenty-four hours.

At home, my wife will put instant coffee in the microwave and tell the machine to "Hurry up!"

We don't want to wait for anything.

When I sit watching television, I have the remote control in my hand and I'm zapping through the channels. I admit it — I have no patience. I want to see a good show and I want to see it now. And if I do find a potentially good show, what do I do? I keep zapping — there might be something *better* on someplace else.

I don't think I'm that different from the rest of us.

In America in the nineties, we don't want to wait for anything. We want it instantaneously. We've become a nation of people who consistently use instant mixes, overnight delivery, supersonic jets, cellular phones, and condensed books.

That's fine, but it doesn't work that way with goals.

It doesn't work that way with enrichment. If something is important enough to be a goal, if something is important enough to warrant an investment of your emotional energy in it as a goal, it's also important enough to give it a realistic time-frame for achievement.

Let's take another example. I really love golf. Given the chance, I'll head for the golf course in a heartbeat. I watch the tournaments on television, and I dream of being another Jack Nicklaus or Arnold Palmer so I can win on the PGA Tour.

One of my personal goals is to become a really good golfer. This is realistic. I'll be able to shoot close to par someday if I practice and work at it. This is realistic.

To say though that my handicap will magically vanish and I'll shoot par next weekend (even though I haven't had time to play a round of golf in the last month) is totally unrealistic.

If I set shooting par this weekend as a goal, I'm going to get discouraged — so discouraged I may give up altogether. However, if I say I'll set my goal to take a lesson every week so I can improve my swing and help my putting, then I've given myself a target to shoot for that's reachable.

Set your goals to be realistic and attainable. If you're six foot three, don't waste time yearning to be a jockey. If you hate math and dislike physical sciences, don't set your goal to be an architect. If you'd rather take a beating than go in the kitchen and cook a meal, don't set your sights on becoming the next Julia Child.

Dan Dierdorf put it well when he said: "If I've got correct goals, and if I keep pursuing them the best way I know how, everything else falls into line. If I do the right thing right, I'm going to succeed."

Before we meet again tomorrow, I want you to start looking at your mission priorities and your trade-off commitments.

Begin to construct two separate goals — one that relates to your personal life and one that relates to your career. You may have many more goals than this before you're through, but for now I want you to just concentrate on two — one personal and one professional. If you're retired, pick a goal that relates to some area of your life outside yourself and your family. It might be refer to doing volunteer work or building an entrepreneurial business or expanding a hobby.

Make sure these goals are very specific — no generalities allowed.  And, make sure that they are very realistic, both in terms of who you are and how you live — and the amount of time you are able to devote to achieving them.  Set yourself up for success instead of failure.

**DAY 7**

# Setting Your Goals,
# Part Two

Today we will complete the first half of our fourteen day process called "Just Say Yes! — A Step Up to Success." You are still collecting puzzle pieces that will come together to make the picture of an enriched and fulfilled future for you and your family.

We have been talking about the importance of setting goals and the five criteria that every goal must meet if it is to be successful. Yesterday, I asked you to set two goals for yourself — one personal and one related to your profession or outside interest. Did you do that? And, did you write those goals down in your workbook? I hope so. As you'll learn during today's session, writing down your goals is one of the most important steps you'll ever take.

I'd like to get started right away with the next criterion of an effective goal. We've seen that goals need to be specific and they need to be realistic.

The third test of an effective goal is that it must be *congruent.*
What do I mean by congruent?
If I use the dictionary definition, you'd hear that congruence means the state of being in agreement or coinciding. When two things are congruent, they are alike. They don't fight each other. They are in alignment.

We talked a little about this earlier in the process, but it's worth repeating. Your goals have to relate to your priorities — which are, in turn, linked to your values.

Remember, the major priorities are Enrichment, Individualism, Power, Structure, Altruism, and Economics, with each having a ranking from one to six in order of their importance in your life. This is why you have to find a way to structure your work goals and

your home goals in a way that they fit into your priority ranking.
Why?

Because if you don't, they won't motivate you and you won't feel fulfilled even if you achieve the goals that you set.

I guess the closest analogy would be to a machine in which every part must work together if the engine is to function.

If your car has new tires and new brakes but the battery isn't charged, you're going to sit in the garage.  If your spleen and your kidneys and your liver are fine but your heart isn't working, you're not going anywhere.

Here's another example.  Let's say that the chief priority that you identified earlier is Structure. You depend on the rules. You like doing the right thing. You find freedom in discipline and you value a high-degree of personal and self-discipline.  But yet, as you look at your goals, every one of them is Economic.

Even if you achieve all the financial goals that you have, but you didn't work within a defined structure to reach your goals, you're going to feel that something is missing.

On the other hand, let's say your goals are Economic and that is your primary motivation — to earn more money and be able to build a sound financial base and to accomplish good through accumulated wealth.  That is the priority that you hold most dear.

However, a check of your day shows you spend a significant amount of your time on the Sunday School board and working with the PTA instead of making money.

Even if you become the best Sunday School teacher in the world,  it's not going to be important to you unless you are making more money doing it.

What happens is that the disagreement between what we're trying to do and what we need to do is like two gears that are out of mesh.  They grind against each other instead of moving together smoothly to move the machine forward.  When they've been worn down enough, they stop turning altogether and freeze.  That's what we do when we try to fight our natural proclivities.

The point is, your goals and priorities have to be congruent. They don't have to be exactly the same but  they have to complement one another.  If your goals are not congruent with your priorities, you're not going to feel enriched.

The fourth element of an effective goal is that it be *balanced.*

As you go through the process of formulating your goals, it's very important to realize how important balance is to the equation. The challenge is to find a way to balance your life, your values, and your priorities.

I've worked with a lot of people during goal setting processes. We go step-by-step through the process of identifying their goals and when we look at the result, all the goals are professional. They all relate to the world of work or to making more money.

Then the person will look at me and say, "I just don't understand why I'm not fulfilled."

That's like saying: "I know all the weight is on one side of the canoe but I can't imagine why we're tipping over into the water."

If your goals are all in one area of your life, then you're just like that badly loaded canoe.

Your whole achievement is going to be in one area of your life and, by default, that means other areas are going to suffer. If you give up your personal life for a few months — or even a year — so you can devote more time to building a business, then you'll be okay.

But, if you center your entire existence around your work and give up all other activities, you may be nominated for "workaholic of the year"...and you'll burn out. No accomplishment will really satisfy you because you won't have anyone to share it with. You've got to make the time to stop and smell the flowers.

Now, there are going to be periods when you encounter exceptions to this rule. Say you're an accountant. Around April fifteenth, you're going to be pretty unbalanced in terms of time devoted to professional versus personal goals. If it's December and you're in the retail business, your personal goals will have to take a back seat to the necessity of keeping the store open for holiday shoppers. If a family member is seriously ill, you may have to spend twenty-four hours a day tending to strictly non-business activities. However, these are all temporary situations.

Taking a defined period of time and temporarily upsetting the balance is okay. The danger comes when you don't re-adjust the load and get the canoe upright and floating again.

Let's take a closer look at how you can do this.

I said you have to have goals for your work and for your home.

Obviously, goals for your work are easy to understand. We all have work goals. You may want to be promoted to the management position that's opening up in your department or change careers or start your own business. Those are easy.

The home goals are also fairly simple to understand. Whether you live in a one-room apartment or a twelve-room home, you have projects you want to get done. There's always a room that should be painted or a redecorating project or gardening that's overdue or a garage to be cleaned out. Setting those goals won't take you very long.

Goals you set for family and friends are a different issue. These usually center on your relationship with the people who are central to your life. Your family goals might include ending an estrangement with a parent or sibling — or you could have the goal of spending more time having fun with your children or courting your spouse all over again. You might want to have a goal of spending one day a month doing something together as a family unit or putting up the basketball hoop so you and the kids can shoot baskets before dinner every night. Your goal may be a family plan for saving money so you can take a special trip together next summer.

Where your friends are concerned, these goals are also centered on your relationship with them. Many times, we become so centered on one area of our lives that we neglect our friendships. Friends are the family we choose instead of the family we are given and those friendships must be nurtured and tended to if they are to flourish.

The author of *The Prophet*, Kahlil Gibran, said: "A friend is your needs answered." You may need to set some goals aimed at allowing you to spend more time with your friends. If your address book is slim, then you need to find new ways to meet more people. Most major newspapers have a listing of various activities in your town that center on specific interests. Find something that intrigues you and attend a meeting. Take an adult extension class. Get out of your house or office and expand your circle of friends.

And then, there are the purely personal goals. Now, obviously all the goals we've just talked about affect you in one way or another but purely personal goals are a different matter entirely.

These are the goals you set only for yourself. These are what might be called the selfish goals — and I'm using "selfish" in the best sense of the word — relating to "self."

If you are to love and care for others — if you are to be effective and productive in your world — you have to love and care for yourself first. Too often, we take time for everyone but ourselves.

I have a friend who has owned a wonderful piece of exercise equipment for almost a year but she works so hard for her clients — often up to fifteen hours a day — that she never has time to use it. She puts her own needs at the very bottom of her list of priorities. Meanwhile, even though her office is in her home, the NordicTrack® sits in her living room, undusted and unused.

This is a good time to do a personal inventory. It's too simple to set the customary goals of losing weight and getting more exercise. Dig deep and think of some of the other things you'd like to do for yourself. Maybe you want to learn a new skill — like scuba diving or woodworking or calligraphy.

Perhaps you want to change something about your teeth or your body. Maybe it means wearing braces for a couple of years or having some minor plastic surgery. Identify what you want for yourself alone. It could be as simple as a new wardrobe in an entirely different style than you usually wear or changing the color and cut of your hair. It might be as major as moving to another part of the country or changing your lifestyle from a farmhouse in the country to a loft in the heart of downtown.

Whatever your personal goal is, center on it.

Until you know what you want and prepare yourself to get it, the other goals won't happen — or if they do, they won't carry with them the satisfaction they should.

Another part of balance concerns the number of goals we set for ourselves. In the first flush of this process, it's easy to get carried away. Goals become like New Year's Resolutions. The list goes on and on — so many that we end up never doing any of them. There are so many options that we become discouraged. Even though in grade school we learned that the way to eat an elephant is "one bite at a time," as adults we become overwhelmed by long lists of "should-do's."

While I don't recommend a lengthy list, there are exceptions to the rules. I've heard that Lou Holtz, the Notre Dame football coach, took out a sheet of paper and wrote down two or three hundred things he wanted to do in life and he started checking them off as he set his goals to achieve them. But, I think that's often the exception instead of the rule — especially for those of us who are just getting started on the work of enriching our lives.

I want you to build a momentum of achievement instead of trying to do too many things at once as we go through this process. That's why I've asked you to isolate only two goals to begin with — one personal and one professional.

Later, when you are more comfortable with the goal setting procedure, you'll need to look at the priorities that you've defined as important to you and understand what's most important to you.

Ask yourself: "What are the three things I'd like to accomplish professionally, at work? What are three things I'd like to accomplish at home or personally that are going to help me enrich my life?"

You are the only person who can answer those questions and your answers will profoundly affect the quality of the rest of your life.

I encourage you to keep your goal list at no more than six major goals at any one time. Remember, goals will change and you may set new goals to replace others that are no longer as significant as you thought they would be. You will also learn that every major goal has minor "sub-goals," if you will, which help you attain your objective. We'll be talking about them tomorrow on Day Eight.

Your goals have to balanced. You have to have goals for your work and goals for your home. You have to have goals for your family and friends and you have to have goals for what you want for yourself, personal goals. You have to plan for the ebb-and-flow of life commitments and be ready to rearrange your life after the special commitment is over. Every element in the picture has to be balanced and compatible. Growth has to happen personally and professionally.

The final — and perhaps the most important — element of an effective goal is that it has to be *written.*

A written goal is a contract with yourself. When you commit your goals to paper, you take them out of the realm of the ephemeral and unreal and you make them concrete and reachable.

That contract with yourself can drive you to achieve great things but writing them down isn't enough. It won't do you any good if you write out your goals in a notebook and then put it in the drawer.

Don't put them in a file hidden on your hard drive. You've got to keep them visible and in front of you all the time. Our minds tend to focus on what we focus on. Earl Nightingale's "Strangest Secret" says it clearly: "We become what we think about."

One of the problems I had to overcome was that I tend to keep a messy desk. I like to believe the sign that says a "messy desk is a sign of genius." If that is true, I should be getting a Nobel Prize any day now!

At any time, there were so many things to concentrate on, all piled up on my desktop, that it was difficult to get anything done — until I developed the habit of just keeping in front of me what I was working on. I learned the great advantage of concentration.

General Patton said: "You must be single minded. Drive for the one thing on which you have decided." He certainly proved how well concentration worked for him.

James Allen, who wrote the classic motivational book, *As a Man Thinketh*, said that concentration "...is a process of diverting one's scattered forces into one powerful channel."

And, the golf great Arnold Palmer describes how he wins tournaments. His description of concentration is "... focusing totally on the business at hand and commanding your body to do exactly what you want it to do."

What you've got to keep in front of you — what you've got to concentrate on — are just the goals that you're setting. Nido Qubein is an internationally acclaimed professional speaker who is generous with his time and known for getting projects accomplished. Nido says: "Nothing can add more power to your life than concentrating all your energies on a limited set of targets."

I've been pleased and proud to be on the platform several times with Arnold Schwarzenegger. We've had the opportunity to talk at some length, and I learned that Arnold Schwarzenegger set goals early in his lifetime. He decided to become the greatest bodybuilder in the history of the world.

Now, if you're a young man growing up in Austria and you become the greatest body builder in the history of your *nation*, I think the human tendency is to say to yourself: "Well, that's really what I meant. I'm tired of pumping this iron. I'm sick of working out. I really meant I was going to become the greatest bodybuilder in the history of my country."

But, Arnold had written down these words on this note card: "I want to become the greatest bodybuilder in the history of the world." He had made a contract with himself. You can break contracts with other people. You can renege on a promise but you can't break a contract with yourself. It would be like cheating at Solitaire — what's the point?

He told me it was the specific listing of his goals that drove him — he says almost forced him — to go to Los Angeles and start the climb to become Mr. Olympia.

So, the challenge becomes to keep your goals narrowed to those most important and keep them in front of you. I have five things written down that I plan to accomplish in the next five years. I keep them written on a card that I have taped to the bathroom mirror.

Why? Because I want them to be the first things I focus on in the morning. I also put them on a little card I laminated so I can keep it in my wallet. I pull it out several times a day and re-read the list.

Sure, I've got every comma memorized but it is a powerful trigger to see the words in front of me over and over again. A quick read-through while I'm waiting for a plane or paying for lunch or putting away a receipt can give me an immediate jolt of renewed vigor. It reminds me what I'm working for and keeps me moving in the right direction.

The reason you want to keep your goals in front of you is that you want to maintain a high level of focus. You want to stay centered on what's really important — and let's face it, if something is important enough to be considered as a major goal, then it must be important enough to focus on and devote time to and write down as a contract with yourself.

This is the point where another issue comes into play — that most terrifying word of our time — "commitment." Nothing commits you to a project quite as much as writing it down.

I think this is part of the reason we've become a culture of telephone communication — somehow, if you can't see the words, they aren't as binding. Even most regular FAX paper communications fade out after a few weeks.

There was a time in our history when a person's word was as good as a lawyer-drawn contract. Those days are long gone. We live in the era of signing on the dotted line — and trips to court for the slightest infringement of a written promise. Our obsession with broken commitments keep lawyers in business.

When you look at your written goals, you'll find it much more difficult to shift and change them on a whim.

If you get discouraged, you won't be so ready to it shrug off and forget it — or settle for lowered expectations. I feel so strongly about this self-contract idea that I even formally sign my goal list so I really feel it is binding. Somehow, nothing is quite as important to us as our own signature. Try it. You'll see what I mean.

Besides commitment, the other objection that I hear when I advise people to write down goals is: "I don't want anyone else to know. My goals are private. I hate that section in my day planner that wants me to write down my goals — they're no one else's business. If everyone knows what I want for myself, they'll laugh at me if I can't accomplish them."

I can't argue with the those sentiments — I've felt them myself — but listen carefully to what is being said. We want to keep our goals private because we don't want to be found out if we fail.

We have no faith in our own abilities so we are afraid to be honest about our plans for our future. We worry that our friends will think we're trying to do more than we should. We're aiming too far above our capabilities.

When the poet, Robert Browning, said: "Man's reach should exceed his grasp, else what's a heaven for?" he was telling us that it's okay to try and touch the stars.

If you're uncomfortable advertising your goals, keep them in private places. Don't put them on the mirror in the bathroom if the family will see them. Instead, tape them inside your sock drawer or on the steering wheel of the car only you drive. Every one of us has someplace we go to everyday that is ours and ours alone.

What I'm saying is, there is no excuse I can think of to keep you from writing down your goals and making that special contract with yourself.

Before we get together tomorrow, I want you to go back to your workbook and open to the page where you wrote down your two first goals. You have already checked to make sure they are specific and realistic. Now, I want you to check them against your priority list.

Are your goals congruent with what is important in your life? Do they provide an extra measure of balance to your existence? Have you written them down on a separate piece of paper — and then signed the paper so you have a binding agreement with yourself?

Tomorrow, we're going to look at an important component of goal fulfillment — objectives. For you to really benefit from this next step up to success, you have to be very sure that you know exactly what it is that you want.

Don't take any shortcuts. You will need to refer back to your workbook often in the days — and the weeks and months — ahead.

# DAY 8 | Goal Objectives

I hope you have your two goals in front of you so you can keep them clearly in your mind. Have you made sure that they conform to the qualities of an effective goal — that they're specific — realistic — congruent — balanced and written?

Good! Then it's time to move on to Objectives.

If you're like most people, something you may have noticed as you went through the goal setting exercises is that there is a sense of exhilaration. Suddenly you're full of energy and eager to get started.

"Boy, now I've got a plan. I've got a road map for life. It relates to my priorities. These goals make more sense than any goals I've had in the past." While that feeling of euphoria is great, I've found it often passes very quickly when it meets up with the cold light of reality.

It's replaced by a feeling of: "Oh my goodness, this is overwhelming. I've gone and committed myself to some heavy-duty stuff here. If I don't achieve it, I'm going to feel like I'm a failure."

If you've ever bought a house, then you're familiar with this sensation. There's the thrill of getting the loan and then, as soon as you sign the mortgage, all of a sudden you're overcome with panic. Or, you've ordered a new car with all the bells and whistles and options. You wait for it and anticipate it and then, when you drive it off the lot, the fright sets in. There are payments to make and insurance to pay and paint that can get scratched. The thrill changes into thoughts of: "Oh my gosh, what have I done?" In psychology, it's called "post-purchase dissonance." Sales people call it "buyer's remorse." It's that bad feeling you get after you buy something you really want but secretly don't think you deserve.

It's no different with goals. First, we set our goals through this 14-day process and then there's the discomfort we go through afterwards. "Did I set my goals properly? Did I do the right thing? Maybe I could have chosen a goal that is more important or significant. Did I think too much about me and not enough about other people?"

Don't worry!

These are all natural responses to what you're doing right now. If you stick to the program, it won't be long before you'll be able to change your discomfort into anticipation and your fear into a challenge.

The tools we're going to use to accomplish this are the objectives. Objectives are what break our goals down into meaningful, manageable and achievable steps. They are the best way I know to get past the feeling of being overwhelmed. They are the blue collar components of our goals. By that I mean that they make us stop, get out of the planning mode and get down to work. They move us beyond the dreaming phase — the "gosh I want to" phase — and take us to the point of actually doing what we need to do if we're going to get the job done.

Today we're going to break down your major goals so that you have a list of objectives that will make the goals real and workable.

For example, say your personal goal is to buy a new house. You have made this goal specific. You want a white colonial in a safe suburb with an easy commute. You need three bedrooms, two baths and a yard for the kids. Ideally, you'll have a space where you can expand later if the family needs the extra room — and you want a yard big enough for the kids to play safely and you can build a deck with a barbecue.

You've made certain that this is a realistic dream. You've scouted out the areas and found where you can buy a home like this in your price range — maybe with a little stretch. The commute will be reasonable and you'll have friends and family nearby.

This goal is also congruent with your current priorities and lifestyle. The area has an excellent adult education program through the local college so you can continue your studies. Your spouse will be able to volunteer at any number of organizations to benefit the community.

Owning this house will give you even more balance in your life because you'll be able to spend more time at home. You'll be working towards a future that has definition.

You've also written all the things you want to have — even putting a picture of what you want your dream house to look like on the bulletin board over your desk so you see it every day and keep it uppermost in your thoughts.

That's all great — but do you have any idea of how you're going to go about getting this house? Where are you going to begin? Here's where we start lining up objectives. After we set that big goal of having a new home, we're going to have to break down what we're going to have to do to have that new home into a series of sub-goals. These are the small steps — the baby steps, if you will — that it will take to eat that elephant one bite at a time.

If you want to move into a new house, you have to make a list of short-term objectives you have to reach. For instance, you're going to have to arrange financing. You're going to have to make sure you pay your bills so you don't have an outstanding debt that is too large on your credit cards. You have to check your credit records and clear up anything that could be an impediment to getting a mortgage — and you have to prepare a financial statement to prove your ability to pay.

Then, you have to take a look at what the varying finance rates at banks and S&Ls and different local institutions and pick up loan applications. You have to determine what you can afford to pay and make some decisions about what size mortgage you're going to apply for.

And, still you're not done. You have to choose a Realtor — look at houses until you find one that meets your needs — arrange to sell your current house — the list goes on and on. But, each of these steps is an objective — a sub-goal — that will carry us towards the ultimate goal.

If you want to visualize what an objective is, think of it as a kind of middle man between what we normally do on a daily basis and our goals. Our goals are the big picture. The objectives are the brush strokes on the canvas. Individually, they aren't particularly meaningful. Seen together, they create a thing of beauty.

I like to think of it as being like a rocket ship blasting off. The rocket is designed to ignite in stages. As each stage is activated, it moves the astronauts further along in their mission. You've got the astronauts in their capsule on top of the rocket. That's where you are. And below you, you have all of these rocket stages. The first rocket takes it off. When that is done, what does it do? It drops away and allows the next stage to kick in. There are some long stages and some short stages but they all work towards the same end.

It's the same process with objectives. Financing the home is a big stage and you break it down into shorter stages. As you accomplish the shorter stages, they'll drop away, allowing another stage to kick in, moving you closer to your goal.

One of the ways you process objectives is through questions. You need to continually ask yourself questions to refine and develop this process.

It's important to note at the outset that these questions are *not meant to be negative.* They aren't supposed to challenge you and show how ridiculous your dream is. They are information-gathering questions, very similar to the questions every budding reporter is taught to ask — though not quite in the same order. Basically, you need the answers to: "what, why, who, when and how?" And then you add one more trigger question: "And then what?" I'll show you how this works.

Let's go back to our house example. We'll just look at the economic aspect of this goal. The first question you ask is: "What do I have to do?" You have to find financing. "Why is this necessary?" Because if you can't borrow the money for the mortgage, you can't buy the house. "Who needs to be involved in this phase of the process?" You and one of the lending institutions.

"When do I have to get this done?" As soon as possible. There's no sense spinning your wheels until you know you qualify for a mortgage. And then, "How will I arrange the financing?" You'll survey different banks, S&L's and other lenders and find out what the interest rates are, and where you can make the best deal.

This is where that extra question comes in: *"And then what?"*

After you figure out where the best deals are, you probably ought to pick up loan applications at a couple different places just for back-up. "And then what?" You better get your personal finances in order and find out how much you can afford to spend.

The process continues on and on and on, continually narrowing the scope of the tasks that have to be completed and honing in on your ultimate goal.

You continue breaking down by objectives until you get to the finest possible point when there are specific steps you need to take, which we'll talk about tomorrow when we discuss daily actions and time-planning.

One of the questions I hear most often is: "How long should these objectives last?" There's no real answer to that one. Objectives can be of varying duration. It all depends on the scope of your goal. If you want to go from being a couch potato to running the Boston Marathon, it's going to take several years. If you want to repaint the garage and set up a work area for yourself, it could take a couple of months. You control the time factor.

I know a couple who own a charming row house in San Francisco. They are working on it themselves as their busy schedules and strained budgets allow. On the ground floor, they took space meant to be storage and have carved out a guest room and bath opening on to the handkerchief-sized garden. It's a little jewel of a room — not very big but designed and built with great attention to detail. They did all the work themselves and it took them seven years to finish it.

Another couple I know had a second story put on their garage so their college-age son would have a place to live where he was home but still had privacy. It took only a couple of months from drawing board through contractors to completion. You set your own timetable.

Objectives last as long as they need to. If your goal is to put four children through college, you may be looking at a twenty year commitment. If it's to write in a journal every day, it may be a lifetime commitment. Remember, because your goals have been tested against the five effectiveness criteria, you know you have a realistic time frame. As you go through listing the individual objectives for each of the components of attaining your goal, understand that there's no time frame attached to the achievement of these objectives at this point.

In fact, I advise that you shouldn't be as concerned about *when* you accomplish your goal. What's really important is that you *do* accomplish it. So don't worry about time right now. Just concentrate on breaking your goals down into manageable activities.

Another concern I often hear is: "How many objectives can I have?" Again, there's no set number. While you want to limit the number of goals, you don't have to limit the number of objectives to achieve those goals. They will vary depending on the goal that you have — whether it's long-term, short-term, how significant it is and how difficult it is to achieve.

There are many variables here but since we're breaking the process down into baby steps, it's okay to have what seems to be a huge number of objectives if that's what it's going to take. The key is to break down the impossible dream into a manageable set of possible activities.

What you want to do is to continue to isolate the objectives, until you can no longer answer the question: "And then what?" without saying: "Now, I'm ready! I'll just do it!"

When that happens, you know you've broken down the objective to the point where it becomes a daily action, which is the next phase we'll be working on during Day Nine.

At this point, I want to make very sure that you understand that while these questions are not negatives, you should be prepared to hear a lot of negative comments from other people while you go through this process. As you start developing objectives and implementing your workable system for success, you're going to have some nay-sayers.

These are the people who want to hold you back and keep you from achieving — not because they don't like you but because they haven't taken the positive steps you have to succeed.

No sooner will that negative someone see that you have this book than you're going to hear them say: "What silly scheme have you got going now? Why did you spend your money on a self-help program? You could have used that cash for something else?"

As you get into the process, you'll get excited about the changes that are happening in your life. You'll suddenly have a new purpose for living and goals to achieve. You have a reason for existing and a future that promises to be rich and fulfilling. This will make you the perfect target for every cynical and negative person you know. There is no better way to be set up as a bullseye than to work on getting out of the rut you're in. All your rut-mates will view you with resentment. You must prepare for that so you don't get distracted from the path you're now walking.

The reason this will happen is that, unfortunately, it's easier for people to criticize your efforts than to go to work for themselves. You'll learn there's a difference between a question to obtain information and a negative assertion. By that I mean, there are some people who are going to say, "That's great! How are you going to swing it?" There's someone who wants information.

And then, there's the other response! "You want to do what? How are you think you're ever going to accomplish that?" In that case the implication is that there's no way in the world you'll be able to do it. The trick is to make sure you don't fall into that second negative category when you're asking yourself the questions.

You're trying to get information in the objective-establishment process. You're trying to get you to think of the next step. *How* will you. . . ? *What* is the process that you will use? *Where* do you have to go next? *Who* can help you? *What* is the step that you'll take to do that next thing? *And then what*?

I remember when I was growing up, I was often asked by my Mom. "What are you going to do today, Scott?" I'd tell her I was going down to the store to help Dad for a couple of hours.

That wasn't good enough. She'd come back with: "And then what are you going to do?" Well, Mark and I are going bike riding. "And then what?" She needed to make sure that I was getting my work done and getting enough exercise and playtime and still getting my chores done at home on the farm. Her goal was to raise me to be a responsible and healthy adult. To do that, she had the daily objectives of making sure everything I did led me towards her ultimate goal. At the time, I didn't understand but today I bless her for it!

So when you ask: "And then what?", it's not a challenge to yourself. It's not a negative assertion. It's a way to get you to refine your objectives, to continue breaking them down.

The problem for most of us is we'll focus our attention only on the goals. It would be like looking at a travelogue of Paris. You see the Eiffel Tower and the Champs Elysee, the parks and the river and the shopping and the museums and you want to go there. Your eye is on the big picture — the ultimate goal. You can taste it and smell it and hear it — but the fact is, you can't just get up and leave your house tonight and go to Paris without doing some preliminary work.

Your goal may be set — but you have to get a passport, arrange for the time away from work or home, buy tickets, pack your bags, make reservations for a place to stay, get traveler's checks and on and on and on.  When you look at Paris this way, it may seem a little farther away but it's much more reachable.

Remember, I said earlier that enrichment comes from the progressive achievement of a goal.  The happiness and enrichment you're looking for in your life isn't going to be found at the destination.  It's going to be found in the journey.

This is where the get-rich-quick programs always seem to fail because what they tend to do is focus on the end destination and not on the step-by-step-by-step plan.  It's the methodical working towards a defined end that has truly made people rich and successful.  If it's going to happen, it's going to happen because of a well-crafted plan.

Business leaders tell me, entrepreneurs tell me — and I know from my own experience — that when you go to try to borrow money for business, lenders don't look at the goal.  They want to see the business plan.  They want to see how you've broken it down.  Banks and financial institutions want to see the steps and they want to know what you've done — and what you're planning to do — to make this dream a reality.

There's no get-rich-quick scheme here.  What the **Just Say Yes!** program gives you is a blueprint you can follow.  Your enrichment will be built step-by-step so it's going to last and it's going to be there for a long time.

Do you ever buy lottery tickets?  Sheri and I do sometimes — when we remember — but we don't count on winning.  Same thing with visiting Las Vegas or Atlantic City.  For some of us, the only way you get rich quick is through winning at some gamble.  My response to that is that there's even a plan — a set of objectives, if you will — that have to be carried out in gambling.

Take the magazine sweepstakes!  Ed McMahon doesn't just call your home and say, "Hey, congratulations!  We've never heard of you but you've won!"  No way!

You have to make an effort to wade through the never-ending envelopes delivered to your mailbox.  You have to find and paste and send back on time.  It's really rather complicated and, if you look at the process, you'll find there's even a step-by-step plan to follow over the course of the contest.

So what we're trying to do here is get the big goals broken down into meaningful objectives — and that's the next thing I want you to do in your workbook.

You're going to make organizational charts — very much like the example you see here in the book. You want to make one for each goal — your professional and your personal. At the top, in a box, put your goal. Then, draw a line down and put another box. In that, put a major sub-goal or objective. Radiating down from that sub-goal will be other objectives. I usually make a list of all the objectives and then put them into the chart, so they are in chronological order — the first things I have to do are at the bottom and the ultimate goal is at the top. You may like to work sideways with the goal at the right and the objectives flowing out to the left. It's your chart and you should develop the system that will be most meaningful for you.

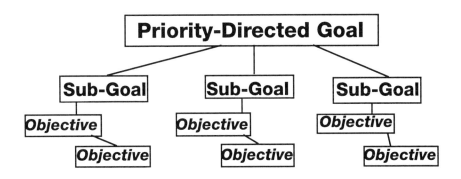

You may want to get a bigger piece of paper and make yourself a wall chart. I've done that for big goals. I list every possible little objective I can think of — and I buy a set of bright-colored markers and cross off each step as I accomplish it.

I had a friend in college who would take a chain of paper clips and for each class, use one paper clip for every book that had to be read or assignment that had to be handed in. He got very creative. Bigger paper clips meant major papers or tests. Smaller ones were for less significant assignments. Each clip had a tiny piece of paper on it identifying its purpose. As each task was completed, the paper clip was taken off the chain.  By the end of the semester, the chains were gone — and my friend was usually carrying home an "A."

He'd found a system that worked for him and I want you to do the same for your goals.  We're now at the point where we're taking something that was just a dream eight days ago and making it into a real project that can be attained.

Make out your objectives charts and we'll meet tomorrow to talk about daily actions and time planning.  See you then.

# DAY 9
# Daily Actions and Time Planning

I wish I could look at each of your Objective Charts and see how you worked out the steps you need to take if you're going to reach your goal. Wasn't it an interesting — and enlightening — exercise? I always find myself amazed by what I have forgotten that needs to be done.

Again, a word of caution. It's easy to look at your carefully laid out plan of attack and assume that since the objectives are neatly listed, they've already been accomplished.

It's like the person who buys a self-help book, carries it home, leafs through it and puts it on the bedside table. They never touch the book again — but if you ask, they'll tell you they're reading it — and then wonder why it hasn't affected their lives in a positive way. The list of objectives is just that — a list, a guideline, a road map. Now the work begins.

It bears repeating that if you look at the Bible — which, religion aside, is one of the best self-help books ever written — you'll see that it's not a book of goals but it certainly is a book of Acts.

The writers of the Bible make it very clear that it's what you *do* that really counts.

That's really the grounding of this program because when you take actions that are in harmony with your value priorities, then you're going to feel enriched and you're going to be successful.

Now we've come to a very critical step in this process. What *are* you going to do? You've been through the initial planning. This is the time when you focus, taking each of the action steps that you've outlined. To you, nothing is more important at this point than to translate the plan that you made into the daily actions that you take.

You've seen how we can be programmed — or allow ourselves to be trapped — by permitting others to choose our daily actions for us. Usually, these are actions that don't reflect our priorities, our goals, or our objectives.

As you've delineated your objectives more and more precisely, you've gotten closer to things you have to do today. I'll go so far as to say if you can't tell me what the first action is that you're going to take today, then you don't really have goals. What you have are dreams. You have wishes. You have a handle on something that you think you'd like.

The only way that any of this turns into a truly value-oriented goal, is if it correlates with the daily actions that you take.

So many times we've taught ourselves to expect less than the best. Dr. Robert Rosenthal developed what he called "The Pygmalion Effect" — in other words, we tend to get what we expect to get — instead of what we want. It's pretty rare that your expectations aren't met.

Richard deVos, one of the founders of the Amway Corporation, said: "Life tends to shape itself to meet our expectations."

And, dozens of thinkers from Horace in ancient Rome to the Dean of Positive Thinking, Norman Vincent Peale, have all related similar ideas. We encourage — consciously and subconsciously — the things that we get out of life.

If you consistently say: "Why try? I never win. I'll never live the kind of life I want," then you're right! You don't have a chance — and there's a good reason for it.

You!

You're probably not doing anything to ensure that you get what you want. Therefore, by expecting that you're not going to be successful, everything that you do — or don't do — will help certify your expectations. You become your own self-fulfilling prophecy.

It doesn't matter whether those expectations are positive or negative. You'll get what you think you should because we tend to arrange our actions in such a way that they'll reflect our expectations. Edgar Cayce summed it up. "He that expects nothing shall not be disappointed, but he that expects much — if he lives and uses that . . . day by day — shall be full to running over."

That's why it's so important to do what we talked about in the beginning: to decide that we're going to take control of our lives today and that we're going to take control of our future.

Another factor that often stops us cold in our tracks is that we develop a fear of failure. We become preoccupied with what's going to happen if we fail? You've probably heard a million clichés about failure.

One of my favorites is, "Failure means that you don't get what you already don't have." If I want to have a million dollars and I set out to make the money — and I don't hit my mark of a million dollars — have I lost anything? No, of course not! I didn't get what I didn't have — but I'm probably a good deal closer than I was when I started!

Remember this about the clichés. They've become clichés because they've been said over and over — and the reason they've been said over and over is because they strike a chord of truth in the people who hear them.

That in mind, one of the most important clichés about failure is this: "It's not the failure — it's what happens after the failure that counts."

I have yet to meet a single successful individual, living a powerful, enriched life, who hasn't yet experienced failure. If you haven't failed, you've never done anything.

Denis Waitley has called failure "the fertilizer of success." Psychiatrist David Viscott says: "To fail is a natural consequence of trying. To succeed takes time and prolonged effort in the face of unfriendly odds. To think it will be any other way, no matter what you do, is to invite yourself to be hurt and to limit your enthusiasm for trying again."

So part of what we have to understand is we can't let the fear of failure paralyze us. As Malcolm Forbes put it: "Failure is success — if we learn from it." What we have to understand is that with our flexible, workable system for success, failure is okay. We just retrench and retool and go at it again.

Failure in an effort is not *failure as a person*. Keep in mind that it's okay to fail in an effort. The essential point is that we have to keep coming back. If we stop coming back and if we stop that effort, then...and only then...do we fail as a person.

Mike McKinney is the owner of a professional speakers bureau and a good friend of mine from Louisville, Kentucky. Mike and I have a line that we keep saying over and over as we confess to each other the current failures in our lives. It relates to fishing because Mike and I have been fishing a couple of times and we've realized that there's only one way that you're going to end up catching fish.

You've got to keep casting. You've got to keep throwing the bait out there.

You know, the fish aren't waiting to jump into the boat so they can have a bite of bait. We have to keep casting to get the bait out there to them.

Whenever Mike or I fail at something we try, the other one will say: "Just keep casting. You gotta keep casting."

I believe that's one of the most important challenges of life.

You gotta keep casting.

But you know, there's another area of the human psyche that I find fascinating. It's the exact opposite of the fear of failure but it's just as paralyzing — and that's the fear of success. It's a deadly form of self-sabotage.

We all know people who almost make it — then they shoot themselves in the foot. I'd be willing to wager that ninety-nine times out of a hundred, it's an unconscious fear of success that makes us do that.

The fear of success can intrude upon our daily activities. What happens if I *do* achieve this goal? Will people look at me the same way? If I do get this new house, does that mean that I move away from my current neighbors? If I become the manager, will my buddies at the office still like me? If I can afford a better life, will I have to change the way I do things? Maybe I don't want this.

The trick is to look this fear of success in the eye and not let it paralyze us. Understand that in any successful situation, things are going to change. For that matter, in any *un*-successful situation, things are going to change. Remember, at the outset of this program, we talked about change being the only constant. We're going to go through change no matter what, so we might as well manage and control that change to the best of our abilities. So, as you look at change in your daily actions, you have to understand that you are in control of your actions and the results are up to you.

One of the most intriguing lessons I ever learned as an adult was that nobody can make you do anything you don't want to do.

You're not a child anymore. Oh sure, your boss can tell you to do something that you may not necessarily enjoy, but if you do it, it's because you choose to. We live in a society governed by laws — but we choose to obey them. We decide to get out of bed in the morning. We choose what we want to eat. Zig Ziglar, one of the great professional speakers and motivators, has often remarked that he never accidentally ate anything in his life.

Think about it. No matter how much you hate doing something, you have to make the choice to do it or it won't get done.

This brings us to one of the buzz-phrases of the Nineties: "time-management."

With our appointment books clutched tightly, our laptop computers in our briefcase, and our cellular phone at our ear, we go about our days trying to cram everything we want to do into the few hours allotted to do it. And we're right to be concerned. Our ability to use the time we have is what's going to control our daily actions and determine how well we take charge of what we do each and every day.

Never mind anything else you've heard about time management. The one essential point that I want you to remember is: There's no such thing as time management. That may surprise you but it is, in fact, the case.

There is no such thing as time management.

You can only manage those things over which you have control and you have no control over time. Let me give you an example.

The Federal Deficit may be something that I wonder about and worry about but I can't manage it. I have no control at all over how much money our government spends. The nuclear power plants in the Soviet Union are another issue I am very concerned about but I have no control over those either. There is nothing I can do to change the situation. You may not like the way your company is being run — but you probably can't manage to change that either, unless you're the one in charge.

Time is much the same. It controls us because there is only so much of it. We don't manage it and that's why I prefer to call it "time planning."

The fact of the matter is: I have no more or less time than the President of the United States or the Queen of England or the

Emperor of Japan. When Bill Gates of Microsoft gets out of bed in the morning, he has the same number of hours in his day that I have in mine. Jack Nicklaus and Donald Trump and Ted Turner and Bill Cosby and Nolan Ryan — they all have the same clock face with the same amount of time. Somehow, they've learned to putt better and make money better and make people laugh better and play ball better than I have learned to do in the same amount of time.

What I'm trying to say is: there are always going to be twenty-four hours in a day. There are always going to be three-hundred-sixty-five and one-fourth days in a year. There are always going to be twelve months in a year. You cannot get up tomorrow morning and do anything to manage November better so that it becomes April. All the time management in the world won't give you a thirty hour day — it'll just make it seem that long. It's all outside of your control.

What we can do is practice time planning and control our *action* management.

We *can* manage our daily actions to fit into the time that we have. That's all we can do — manage the activities that fit into the time that we have. It doesn't matter how many hours you have — it's what you do in that period that makes all the difference in the world.

What are you doing today with the time that you have? How well are you planning the hours of your day? I'd be willing to bet that most of us aren't planning our time very well at all.

That's one of the ways this program is different from others you may have read. It's going to help you take that step up to success because we're coordinating what we need to do, to have what we really want.

The way we do this is by classifying our actions.

Everything that we do has a different degree of urgency and a different degree of importance.

*Urgency* refers to those actions that have a time pressure. They need to be done right now.

*Importance*, on the other hand, refers to how vital an action is to achieving our priority-directed goal. If it's important, you have to do it. If it's urgent, you have to do it *now*.

Most of us, in our daily actions, put more time, more effort and more emotional investment into getting the urgent done before the important — and this isn't very surprising.

If your child runs in and says: "Mommy, it's five minutes until baseball practice starts, you have to get me there!" Is that urgent? By golly, it may not move you ahead towards your value-derived goals but it's sure urgent. It needs to be done right now or else it's not going to happen.

And, it's very difficult to look at your child and say: "Now you listen to me! While your baseball game has a high degree of urgency, it does not have a high degree of importance and therefore it doesn't move me toward achieving my priority-directed goal so I'm not budging from this house." Nice try...but we know, in the real world, that isn't going to happen. What the example does do is give you an idea of what I mean when I say we take care of the urgent before the important.

However, too often we let people take advantage of us. They'll indicate that something's urgent to them and expect it to be urgent to you, too. You will often take their burden, especially if you are someone with a high altruistic drive. We say, "Okay, if it's urgent to them it must be urgent to us," so we spend our lives doing other people's urgent activities. We let them plan our agenda.

Are people you work with the same as that child? Do they ask you to drop something important to accomplish something urgent? It's up to you to remember that the most important thing you have to do is: Do the things that are important!

Sounds simple, doesn't it? Sure, but it's very difficult to implement.

The lesson I want to teach you at this point is to say "no." Our daily actions are not only pro-active but also reactive. In other words, we're going to pro-act by moving in the way we choose towards our priority-directed goal. And, we're also going to re-act by saying the word "no" when people urge us to do what's urgent to them before we can say "yes" to what's important to us.

There are four ways we can classify our daily actions.

First: *any action can be low urgent, low important.* That's something we flat-out need to dump or do with a minimum of effort — like watching television. This is easier said than done by the perfectionists and those who fit in high structure priority. Everything must be done perfectly in their eyes — even things that are low urgent and low important — and therefore they waste a lot of their time. Let's make a pact. If it's low urgent and low important, good enough *is* good enough. Okay?

The second daily action classification is: *high urgent, low important.* Usually, I recommend that we get these things done and get done quickly to get them out of the way.

Better yet, try to delegate them to somebody else or practice saying "no." You can try something like this: "I know you need this done right now but I'm sorry. It's not in my action plan. I can't work this into my schedule right now." I'm not saying that you should be unpleasant about it but you do need to take control because no one else is going to do it for you.

The third classification of activities is: *high importance, low urgency.* In some cases, as we plan our daily actions, the things that are high importance, low urgency, are scheduled in a way so we get them done because they're vitally important. We just may not get them done first. That's fine!

The fourth classification encompasses the most important activities — *those that are high urgency and high importance.* If something is important in moving you toward your priority-directed goal — and it also has to be done soon — that is how you want to spend your time. This is the area you're going to plan into your daily actions.

Look at your objectives that you've refined to a point where you know what you can do today. Tell yourself: "All of these are very important or they wouldn't be objectives translated into daily actions. Now the real question is, which has the highest urgency? What do I do first?"

In a nutshell, that's the absolute system for success. You start with your values, work into your value-directed goals, and then break those goals down into objectives. Finally, you rank those objectives so that now you have a list of things you can start doing today.

Obviously, you're not going to be able to do everything on that list right now. So what if you don't get it all done? You'll get some of it done. Remember that we said success is going to come not at the destination but through the journey.

What you've got to do is understand that at least you're starting to get something done. I hear people say: "I want to have it all in life."

It is very important for me to emphasize here: *You can't have it all until you have it some.*

I'll admit that is not a great sentence. However, I would suggest it makes a profound point. Until you take that first step, you're never going to have everything. What you've got to do is move ahead and get past excuses — and move on.

One hint I can tell you is I've found that it's easier to get the unpleasant tasks out of the way early in the day. There are going to be some items on your list that you just don't want to do. As they say, the most successful people don't necessarily do everything better than anybody else — but they're willing to do things that others won't do. They don't procrastinate and they're willing to sacrifice the moment for the lifetime.

I'll confess it — I'm not excited about exercising. Exercise doesn't make me happy. I don't look forward to it. What I've discovered is that I have to exercise in the morning if I'm going to do it at all. By evening, I have my excuse squadron firmly in place and I don't leave the chair.

My wife, on the other hand, looks forward to exercising. She is thrilled by aerobics class, so she rewards herself by scheduling it at the end of almost every day. Why? Because it gives her something to look forward to throughout the day. Different strokes for different folks.

Let's talk about time planning. At the end of every day, I want you to set aside just fifteen minutes to plan what your tomorrow is going to be like.

You might say: "What if I don't get it all done?" Hey, that's okay. At least you're focusing on what's in front of you. As we said earlier, we have to keep in front of us the daily actions that relate to our value-directed goals.

I suggest that you get some kind of day planner. There are any number of excellent systems on the market — or you can make your own with a good software program for your computer. If you're not already using one, spend some time looking through the various options.

One aspect planners have in common is that most of them divide each hour into four blocks so you can plan your schedule in fifteen minute segments. You should begin to write down in there what time you're going to get up and what time you're going to go to bed. Write in the time allotted for exercising and recreation as well as for work. And be specific. Don't just write: exercise. Put down what you're going to do. Seven to seven-thirty: walk to the park and back. Seven-thirty to seven forty-five: shower and dress. And so forth.

I want you to learn to value each minute of your time. Benjamin Franklin said, "If you value life, waste not time; for time is the stuff life's made of." If you plan every activity of your day, you're going to find that you don't waste much time. Each minute is important because it belongs to you. Cherish the minutes and use them the very best way you can. You'll also find you don't put things off because you have an appointment with yourself to get things done.

You also need to make a prioritized list of the daily actions you're going to take. Number them: One, Two, Three, and so on. The Number One activity is whatever is the most vitally important.

In other words, those activities designated high urgency and high importance. This is going to be one of your highest priorities for that day. Your Number Two activity might be something that's either high urgent, low importance or high importance, low urgency. Number Three might be something that's low in both urgency and importance or low in one or the other.

At the end of the day, I want you to check off the actions you've taken. If you don't get everything done that you planned, just move them to the next day. What you want to do is reward yourself when you do make accomplishments.

You might think this sounds like a lot of work and it would be easier to just keep a big to-do list and go through it at your own speed. Something I've learned — and I don't know what the scientific principle is behind it — but it's very compelling to write the tasks down, day after day. If there is an action step that I didn't get done yesterday, I'll write it down. I'll do it tomorrow. If it doesn't get done tomorrow, you have to write it down again for the next day. It's a gentle punishment you give yourself by writing the task down over and over and over. Finally, you'll force yourself to do it if, for no other reason, that you just don't want to write it down again.

Your assignment for today, Day Nine, is to continue to work through the system. Get yourself on schedule in fifteen minute blocks of time. You'll find it'll get a little easier to say: "Oh, I've got to go because I have another appointment." — even though that appointment might be with yourself. As you learn to manage your activities, it's going to give you the process to accomplish your goals.

Before tomorrow, decide what you are going to do first to make it happen. Promise you'll say "no" to the things that are going to take away your time, your talent, and your energy — and say "yes" to yourself. Try to plan your days as far in advance as possible — at least through the end of the next five days that make up the rest of the program.

Keep on working in your workbook and your day planner. When we meet again tomorrow we'll be talking about different action styles and how we deal with others.

# DAY 10 Inter-Personal Action Styles

Welcome to Day Ten of the **Just Say Yes!** A Step Up to Success Process. If you've been doing your workbook assignments every day — and I really hope you have because that's the only way this program will work for you — then you should be seeing some important patterns coming through.

The feedback I get from seminar participants — and others who have gone through the process — is that, by this time, they have begun to have a greater understanding of who they are and why they behave the way they do. There's nothing quite as enlightening as really getting to know yourself for the first time.

Often someone will come up to me and argue that all the paperwork isn't necessary. "Scott, I know myself inside and out. I don't need all this." That's when I go back to William Shakespeare's great line from *Hamlet*: "We know what we are but we know not what we may be." That's true of most of us. We think we know what's going on inside us — but we have no concept of how different our lives can be.

Aldous Huxley said: "There's only one corner of the universe we can be certain of improving and that's our own self." Doesn't that ring a bell in these days when we seem unable to have much effect on the craziness that's going on around us?

Okay, let's get on with discussing about inter-personal styles. Yesterday, we discussed the need for taking daily action and planning our time so we could move forward toward our priority-driven goals. Today and tomorrow, I want to talk about action styles and how you deal with others, because in the long run, your success is very much dependent on how other people see you and respond to you.

There's a basic premise in sales that people buy from other people. They buy most from the salesperson they like and trust — even if the product is not as good.

If you're going to take that step-up to success, you're going to have to work and live with other people. "No man is an island. . ." and that is as true today as it was in 1670 when John Donne first said it in England. Today, our American ethic is based on diverse personalities working together for the common good.

Because we are so different, it's vital that each of us develop the necessary people skills so we can achieve our goals without keeping others from achieving theirs. The goal is to make allies, not enemies.

All you have to do is pick up the newspaper on any morning and you'll quickly see the full range of diversity we manifest. Since everyone has different priority rankings, they have different agendas. You'll find liberals and conservatives; hawks and doves; Republicans, Democrats, and independents; Catholics, Protestants, and Fundamentalists, Jews, Buddhists, atheists, and the whole range of other beliefs that fall between.

Our country encompasses people who are pro-choice and others who are pro-life; those who believe in the death penalty and those who don't; traditionalists, Yuppies, free spirits, environmentalists, the aged and the young; the active and the passive.

There are those who are the same every time you see them and others who are chameleon-like and change as circumstances require. Some of us are aggressive and others are timid. Some are activists and other take the world as it comes.

Some are on the go every minute and need constant stimulation while others are content to sit on the couch and vegetate. Some are family-oriented and others are centered on business.

And, to make it all the more complex, there is constant crossing-over between these groups. Like a kaleidoscope, we are an ever-changing mix of viewpoints, interests and priorities, wishes, dreams, and morals. While we can be loosely gathered under headings, no two people are exactly alike. That's why our mission is to learn to interact with everyone — no matter who they *say* they are or who they *think* they are — or who they *really* are.

As we grow up, most of us learn the Golden Rule — that universal commandment that doesn't actually appear in any Bible. "Do unto others as you would have them do unto you!" Sounds great! We all buy into it — except those cynics who change it to: "Do unto others — *before* they do unto you." Or, those over-materialistic souls who proclaim the Golden Rule is: "He who has the gold, makes the rules!"

Like most Americans, I learned from parents, schools, and churches, and I went out into the world armed with my Golden Rule. I tried it in selling. I tried to give my clients what I would have wanted. They obviously hadn't been listening when they were taught the rule...or else we just didn't want the same thing.

I tried it in romantic situations. I treated the girls I dated with the same kind of treatment I would have liked. It seemed to turn out some of them acted as though they didn't know the Rule either!

The realization I came to is that the Golden Rule is different in spirit than it is in the literal meaning. Since everyone is different, it logically follows that not everyone wants to be treated exactly the way you do. If you are primarily interested in altruistic, social justice issues and I, as a movie buff, want to spend our time together going to films and seeing the stars, it's pretty apparent that the Golden Rule isn't going to work. When I do unto you what I would want others to do unto me, you're going to be bored, disinterested or disdainful...as well as tired of movies!

My belief is what the Golden Rule really means is don't hurt anyone. Don't do anything knowingly that will cause others pain and discomfort — those are emotions no one of us wants.

What you want to do is go out of your way to make others feel comfortable in your presence. In other words, if you are trying to influence someone who hates to "rock the boat," don't ask them to accompany you to a street protest or sign a radical petition.

The trick is to learn how to understand the person we are dealing with — learn how to read a stranger like a book. Family and friends are somewhat easier, but how can you quickly categorize someone you've just met so you can determine what will influence them and what will turn them off? How do you isolate their particular action styles?

There are three main factors we can study to help us understand the inter-personal action styles people use in doing what they do — and these are: Force, Conformity and Flexibility. Let's talk a little about each one.

To judge a person's Force factor, watch how they present their ideas and information. If they're quiet and shy, speaking softly with few gestures or eye contact, they're very likely a Low Force person.

On the other hand, if a person is assertive and outspoken, quickly jumping to the front of the group and taking the lead, you can be pretty sure you're dealing with a High Force individual.

A High Force person will bulldoze right over a Low Force companion. This is very apparent in business meetings. Often one person in the room will be dominant while others may venture an opinion but seem to retreat if challenged. In fact, the Low Force person is not necessarily backing down; they just don't feel a compulsion to aggressively assert their position on an issue.

Or, watch children on a playground. One child will be the natural leader while others follow meekly. Teams have one captain. There will be one boy or girl who will always seem to announce they have the best ideas for what games to play or where to go next to find fun.

Now, High Force doesn't necessarily mean that a person is a bully or unusually argumentative. The High Force personality is generally just self-confident and eager to share his or her views with anyone who will listen.

The second style we can look for in people we interact with is Conformity. Those with Low Conformity like to make their own decisions. They definitely do not conform to what the rest of the group wants to do. They care about others, but they're not about to waver from the path they believe to be the right one. Once they've made up their minds, getting them to change is like moving a boulder from the middle of the road. Depending on the strength of their Force factor, they may be loud and assertive about their feelings — or they may be quietly immovable.

The Low Conformity individual isn't necessarily unfeeling towards the needs and wishes of others. It is simply that they aren't willing to agree with what others want simply because the majority happens to be in favor of a particular course of action.

High Conformity people are much easier to persuade. They tend to bend with the winds of change. You may never know what they're thinking or how they really feel. They may be so accustomed to following the throng that they aren't sure themselves how they feel about any subject. They'll go along with the majority decision.

Their goal is to "make nice." Their own wants and opinions are put in second place behind the good of the team.

The downside of High Conformity is that these people will say whatever you want to hear — and they tell the next person the exact opposite — if that's what they need. In a manager, this can be very disconcerting because it's difficult to get a firm "yes" or "no" to any question. You often have to approach the High Conformity manager as a group so he or she can appease everyone at once.

The third factor of personality you need to study is Flexibility. Flexibility refers to the consistency of a person's actions. Can you count on this person to act the same way in every situation or will they vary to meet the different circumstances? Is this a person you feel you know or is it a person who's like an actor, becoming whomever you want them to be?

The person with a High Flexibility factor is the individual who changes his or her behavior based upon the situation.

We all know someone who has one particular style of acting when they are at work, then change almost like Dr. Jeckyl and Mr. Hyde when it is quitting time. Or, someone who is one way around their professional colleagues, and another around their spouse.

High Flexibility is found in someone who changes how they behave to keep the situation stable. They reflect the person they're with instead of projecting who they are.

Those who have a Low Flexibility factor, on the other hand, are like the Rock of Gibraltar. This is the person who can be counted on to be the same in every situation, no matter what the situation.

When I worked as the Director of Public Affairs and Annual Fund for my alma mater, Franklin College of Indiana, I worked with an individual who is the epitome of Low Flexibility. He was the same way in any situation...totally tranquil, cool and collected. Nothing ever ruffled Jim's feathers.

Naturally, this is admirable in professional situations, yet there was a time I felt sorry for him because of his inability to be spontaneous. One year in the national basketball tournament for small colleges, our team made a half-court shot at the final buzzer to win the game. Calmly and quietly, Jim merely said, "Nice basket," while the rest of the crowd went berserk.

We all know someone who seems to be ALWAYS enthusiastic, or calm, or sad, or sick, or happy, or whatever. The hallmark of Low Flexibility people is that their behavior is constant and consistent.

Jim's Low Flexibility made him someone to count on and very predictable. It also made him unable to enjoy the thrill of the moment.

But, today we're going to concern ourselves with Force and Conformity. We'll talk more about Flexibility tomorrow on Day Eleven.

What I want you to do now is to develop a Personality Graph just like that in the example. In your workbook, copy the two straight lines that are the center of this graph. The Force Line runs horizontally from left to right. Write LF for Low Force on the left

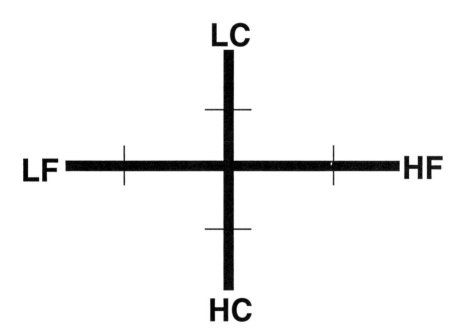

end of the line — and put HF for High Force on the right. The Conformity Line bisects the Force Line, running top to bottom. Write LC on the top of the line representing Low Conformity and write HC on the bottom for High Conformity.

For today, we want to focus on Force and Conformity because these are the backbones of every one of the personality types.

Your assignment for tonight is going to involve drawing this Personality Graph for each of the people you interact with most often so we can discuss how best to use the new insight you'll gain. First, I'd like you to draw a graph for yourself.

Judge where you fall on the Conformity line and put an X to mark the spot. Do you land closer to the bottom with a High Conformity factor because you go along with whatever is being proposed? If so, put your X closer to the bottom of the line. If you always want to change things before you'll agree — if you'd rather lead than follow — put your X closer to the top of the line. Now, do the same for the Force. If you're somewhat quiet without definite views about anything, put your X closer to the left side of the line. If you're usually up on a soapbox, "telling it like it is," your X will go closer to the right. Now, connect these two X's with a straight line so you can see which quadrant you fall into and what your action style is.

Now, in the upper left hand square write "Judicial." In the upper right hand square write "Controller." The lower left hand square should be labeled "Genial" and the lower right hand square should say "Talkative." We'll discuss those designations tomorrow.

The four action styles — judicial, controller, genial, and talkative — aren't original with me by any means. You'll find them in scores of current sales training programs, in the writings of Sigmund Freud, in astrology — and in the works of the early Greek philosophers. Even those venerable old Greeks probably got them somewhere else. You may find the four quadrants with somewhat different names, but they all have similar meanings.

For instance, until the Middle Ages and through the Renaissance, the different personality types were thought to be caused by physical elements within the body. They were called the humors: Phlegmatic, Sanguine, Choleric, and Melancholy. These corresponded to passivity, happiness, anger, and sadness. Other psychologists and trainers have used terms like "analytic" instead of judicial or "facilitator" instead of genial. The point is that the system has been around almost as long as our civilization and has withstood the test of time.

In the **Just Say Yes!** process, we do something that's different. We put a new spin on the four different styles. Yes, we use the Personality Graph as a communications skill and an inter-personal action barometer, but we also use it as a way to improve our aim at goal achievement. The Force-Conformity crosshairs in the center make it easier for us draw a bead on where we want to go.

As you learn to use this graph, you'll find that learning the individual action styles explains a great deal about you and the friends you make. The proverb says: "Bird of a feather flock together" and it's as true as most of the often-repeated expressions we hear.

People tend to like being with people like themselves. It makes you feel good to be with people who reflect your opinions, who act like you act, who respond the way you respond.

The science of Neuro-Linguistic Programming, or N. L. P., also addresses this need to be with similar people. N.L.P. teaches that if you want to persuade people to do what you want, one of the tactics you should use is to mirror what they do. If the person you're talking to crosses their legs, you cross yours. If they lean their chin on their hand, you do the same. If they pick up a pen and take notes, you take notes, too. It makes the other person comfortable and receptive when they see themselves mirrored in you.

Part of this is reflected in the behavior of babies. Give a very young child a mirror to look in and you'll see a perfectly happy little person. In the mirror is someone doing the very same thing that baby is doing and the baby thinks this is the best playmate they could ever have. When we grow up, we still want that reassurance of the familiar facing us in the mirror.

Think of the times you've met someone and felt an instant rapport. You feel as if you've known them all your life. They become friends instantly. This is the basis for that phenomenon called "love at first sight." Usually when it occurs, the couple

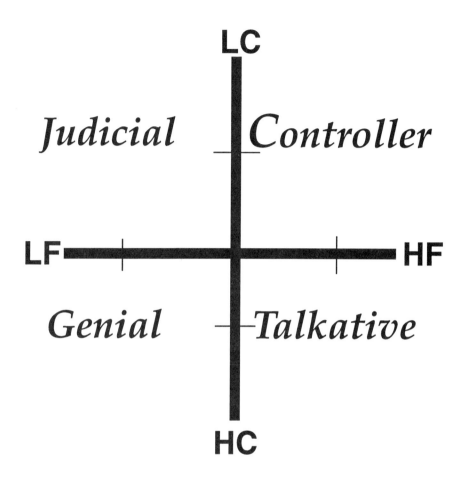

involved are very similar individuals and they feel as if they've known each other forever even though they just met because they are so similar.

One couple I know of decided to get married the first night they met. As they got to know each other better, each said there was very little "getting to know each other" that went on. They were instant friends. It turned out that they had both gone to private boarding schools — and hated it. They'd had the same majors in college. They liked the same music and enjoyed the same sports. Even their handwriting was alike. The immediate compatibility was at least partially due to the similarity of their life experiences. They felt comfortable with each other.

On the other hand, this also explains why some people make us feel awkward and uncomfortable. If the person is radically different, we don't know how to act and react in their presence. "The Prince and the Pauper syndrome" takes over.

If you were raised in a castle, you're going to have a difficult time relating to the person raised on the street. The case could be made that this is the reason for some of the tension between different nationalities and races. The common bond, the rapport, often isn't there between people who have been raised in radically different cultures.

I'm not saying rapport is impossible in this situation. Without the techniques we are going to discuss, however, compatibility becomes incredibly difficult.

We carry this over to the workplace. When we confront a personality opposite to ours in the office, we tend to become defensive. Too often, our unease often makes us shoot ourselves in the foot. We impede our own progress up the career ladder because we don't enjoy our time in the office.

For instance, if you feel comfortable with a boss who builds teams and treats co-workers like family, you're probably not going to be happy working for someone whose style is formal and authoritarian — unless you understand those management differences and don't take them personally.

When you can realize the differences between you and another person, then you can act on the *how* of getting your way instead of the *what* of getting it. You can change the way you approach a situation based on your understanding of the action styles of the people with whom you must interact.

As you'll see tomorrow when we discuss the four different action styles in detail — just like the priorities, there is no "good" or "bad." There is only "different." One of the greatest gifts you can give yourself is to accept these differences in others without being judgmental.

A classic defense mechanism for feeling comfortable when dealing with others who are unlike us is to condemn them. If you prove that they are "wrong," then you become superior in your own mind and that sense of superiority carries you through the unease that can be part of new situations.

I always try to remember the Italian expression that says: "All the world is one country." The truth of that proverb was brought home when I was in college.

A group of us were sitting at dinner, looking at the horrible cafeteria food we'd been driven to by lack of funds. Around the table were several students from foreign countries. As we gamely tried to eat the institutional food — and pooled our money for a possible pizza later — I said: "Better clean your plates. I was always told I had to eat everything because children are starving in Europe." The student from Europe laughed. "I heard they were starving in India!" At which a girl from New Delhi spoke up: "Not at all. My grandmother said children were starving in China." And so it went around the table. Everyone had had the same prodding to eat from anxious relatives. The New Yorker had heard the starvation was in Louisiana. The Floridian was told the famine was in Idaho. The only difference was which state or country had been used as the lever. The whole world really is one country.

A simple childhood admonition would seem to sum up a good deal of what is hurting us in our adult inter-personal relationships.

The grandmother in India was no more right or wrong than my mother in Crothersville or the family in Japan who was sure children were starving in Korea. Not right or wrong — just different.

And, as an aside, any country we could name would have been correct because there are children starving everywhere. Please, make a real effort to be more understanding and less judgmental as you go through the Personality Graphing Exercise.

Every one of us — and I certainly include myself — tends to believe that our way is the right way. Deep down I know that if the whole world would do things the way I do them, then we'd all be just fine! Luckily, I have many people around me who feel it's their mission in life to disabuse me of that idea and to plant my feet firmly on the ground.

The point is, if we're going to be effective, we have to be objective.

Our perception of any situation becomes our reality.  We don't deal with what is real.  We deal with what we *think* is real.

Until 1492, the common belief was that the world was flat.  Of course, it isn't but any map drawn before Columbus sailed to the New World would present it that way.

Then, as now, reality was in the eye of the beholder.

In the everyday world, many of us tend to operate on a "don't confuse me with the facts, my mind is made up" basis.  If a person cannot see the dimension of depth, if only one eye is working or the two eyes don't work together as they should, to that person the world is indeed flat.   They see their environment as if it were a photograph. They can't tell how far away one object is from another. Their perception is two-dimensional and therefore, so is their reality.

Here's a question:  Do you believe the people you work with ALWAYS behave rationally?  If you are married, how about your spouse?  Does he or she ALWAYS behave rationally?

After years of asking this question, the results are 99.9% of people will say that their spouse or colleagues do NOT always behave rationally.

But, the answer is that your associates and spouse, your friends and family members always behave rationally...

*...from their point of view.*

What's the point?  Simply this.  When you know what a person's reality is, you can accept their judgment on the world around them.  In the same way, when you know the personality type of the person you're dealing with, you know how to  interact with them so that you reach a win-win result.

Before we go on and discuss the four personality  types surrounding Force and Conformity — and understand how Flexibility fits into all this, I want you to do your assignment for today.

First, you will make your personal Personality Action Graph. Invest the time in determining where you fall on the cross-bars of Force and Conformity.  Think back on your actions and reactions over the past several months.  How have you responded to various situations?  Have you stood up for what you believe?  Have you gone along with the crowd?  What's your personal style?

Remember, Low Force is on the left side of the horizontal line. Low Conformity is on the top of the perpendicular line.  When you have the proper X's on the two lines, then connect them by drawing a diagonal line from one to the other. You'll see that this line will fall predominantly into one of the four quadrants.

After you've finished your personal graph, choose those people with whom you interact most closely. These can be your spouse, your children, your parents, your boss, your co-workers, your teachers or anyone else with whom you have on-going relationships that will affect the attainment of your goals. Make graphs for them as well.

An interesting insight on this exercise is to have someone you know well plot a Personality Graph on you. You might be surprised at how you appear to other people.

While you may think you are fairly average and fall somewhere in the middle of the graph, your spouse might find you to be High Conformity and Low Force because you're trying to please the significant other person in your life. Your children, on the other hand, might rate you Low Conformity and High Force because you don't give in to their every demand and tend to make your wishes very clear! A friend might say that you're Low Force but Low Conformity because he sees you as someone who doesn't argue very often but also someone who won't let yourself be led around by the nose. He sees you as quietly determined.

Remember, people will respond to your behavior based not upon who you are, but instead upon who they perceive you to be.

Again, I urge you to take the time to write out these graphs carefully. You are nearing the home stretch on the **Just Say Yes!** A Step Up to Success process. The more information you can gather about yourself, the stronger you will be.

Anne Morrow Lindbergh, the author of *Gifts From the Sea*, said that "When one is a stranger to oneself, then one is estranged from others, too." So let's follow Henry David Thoreau's advice from *Walden Pond*. "Explore thyself!"

By the time we meet tomorrow, I expect you to have a much firmer grasp on who you are and how you relate to your world and the people in it.

# DAY 11

# Four Specific Action Styles

Yesterday, we discussed the basic coordinates of the graph, Force and Conformity. At the end of today's session, I'll show you how Flexibility fits into this.

As you charted your Force and Conformity, you noticed that the direct line you drew connecting the X's was primarily in one of the four quadrants.

If you haven't already named the four quadrants, let's do that now. In the upper left hand corner of the graph write "Judicial" and in the upper right hand corner write "Controller." Label the lower left hand corner "Genial" and in the remaining square write "Talkative."

When you look at the diagonal line joining your markings — or those of others you charted — you can see that it falls into one of these four personality types. I want to go through each one of these with you now so you can have a better idea of how you ordinarily behave.

If your line fell in the upper left hand quadrant, you're a Judicial personality. This means you're Low Force and Low Conformity. You don't make much noise — you aren't very verbal about your convictions — and you don't let others make your decisions for you. You are very much your own person. You aren't very impulsive. You require a lot of facts so you can analyze the question. When confronted with any situation, you'll ask to hear all sides, be given the background information, know what the desired result should be — and then you'll churn it all around before reaching a decision.

Judicial people make good computer programmers, accountants, engineers, lawyers, doctors, and debaters. They're very detail-oriented and highly organized. They have a passion for correctness and tend to be perfectionists. They'd rather do nothing than do something that is less than the best.

Because they spend so much time examining the facts, Judicials have a great emotional investment in being "right." They place a high priority on being correct. Just like a Judge, the decisions made by a Judicial tend to be "verdicts." And, once made are very difficult to appeal!

The Judicial types might like Chess but probably won't be happy playing the slot machines. "Luck" isn't in their vocabulary. They earn what they get by working for it methodically.

When the Judicial personality decides to go on vacation, they start planning months in advance. They get out the maps. They confer with travel agents. They call ahead to make sure the reservations have been made and what the weather is like. They make lists of things to do and what will go in each suitcase. Every day is planned out, down to the last detail. There is no chance for error — or spontaneity. There are places to go and people to see and schedules to be met. Money is allotted for each step of the way and unless something unexpected happens, the trip will be a success.

At work, this is the person who loves to write long reports with pages of statistics and graphs. You probably won't find a Judicial in the Creative Department! — unless they're passing through on the way to Research and Development or Accounting. In those departments you'll find plenty of this personality type that you can watch in action.

Classic Judicials I can think of would be President Jimmy Carter; William Gates, the President of Microsoft; Thomas Edison; the English physicist, Stephen Hawking; and, probably at any time, the entire United States Supreme Court.

I love to get directions from Judicial types. Ask me how to get from here to there and I'll say something like "turn right and go one or two miles, then you'll see a corner with a gas station on one side and a strip mall on the other. Turn left and then turn left again right past the seafood restaurant with the neon lobster on top." Ask a Judicial for the same information, and you'll be told to "drive out of the driveway and turn right at the corner. Drive for one-point-seven miles, staying in the left lane. Turn left at the corner of Linden and

Oak and drive another point-five miles," and so forth. They will be logical and precise. Landmarks aren't important when there's an odometer to register exact distances.

These are the strengths of the Judicials. They keep a rein on the rest of us. They're comprehensive and thorough and they keep everyone around them on track.

Their weakness is they can miss important opportunities because they're so busy putting facts together that they never do anything. It's called "paralysis by analysis" and it's the curse of the Judicial personality.

The next style is the Controller. If your diagonal line landed you in the upper right hand quadrant of the graph, you are a High Force, Low Conformity person. You aren't the least bit shy about letting your opinions be known. You are more than willing to set the pace in any contest. You're a natural leader and will avoid following the masses. You're a general but not a foot soldier. You don't take orders easily because you want to be in charge.

The Controller can be domineering, competitive, and aggressive. Decisions are made quickly based on gut instinct. They plunge ahead without too much thought about the side-effects of their actions. Their eyes are fixed on a goal and everyone else had better get out of the way or be sucked into the undertow.

Controllers have a lot of trouble delegating. They subscribe to the Napoleon Bonaparte theory, "if you want a thing done well, do it yourself." They don't feel the need to ask permission of other people before acting because asking for permission is a sign of relinquishing veto power.

Typical Controllers are people like Lee Iacocca who took the Chrysler Corporation from the brink of bankruptcy to solvency. Ted Turner, the man behind the broadcasting empire would certainly qualify, as would most of the CEO's of any Fortune 500 corporation.

It is interesting to contrast the management styles of Controllers and Judicials. Perhaps that's why Roger Smith had so much trouble when he was President of General Motors. He was a highly intelligent man but his background was in accounting. He was a bean-counter — a classic Judicial. All of a sudden he was President of a manufacturing monolith, and one that, given the nature of the car business, was filled with very assertive, dominating individuals.

For example, while Smith was collecting facts, appointing committees and attempting to make reasoned judgments, Ross Perot, then the CEO of EDS — and a classic Controller — jumped in and took GM to the cleaners in a business deal between their two companies.

The strength of the Controller is that they're action-oriented. They're decisive and they're in command of any situation. These are the people who take charge right now and they have little patience with people who they perceive as weak or "wishy-washy."

Their weakness is that they tend not to listen. They are so self-absorbed with their own goals that they don't pay attention to other opinions. It's a case of "Damn the torpedoes — full speed ahead!" Or, "Ready. Fire. Aim!"

If your diagonal line dissected the lower left hand quadrant, you are a Low Force, High Conformity person. You are called a Genial.

You are the most pleasant type of personality to be around. You want everyone to be happy. You want to see people smiling and you want to give others some of the gifts life has given you. You aren't very forceful in your opinions because you don't want to offend anyone. You are willing to go along with the crowd because you don't want to spoil other people's fun. You're the person who'll gag down Mexican food, even if you hate it, instead of suggesting the gang go to an Italian restaurant instead.

The Genial person is usually compassionate and giving. You feel for other people and probably get very emotional when confronted with another's pain. You like to build teams.

Your general attitude is like the old Mickey Rooney-Judy Garland movies where the stars exhort all the kids to get together and clean out the barn so they put on a show. You get to Broadway by building a team to work together — as opposed to the Controller who would be sitting in the Director's chair, barking orders — or the Judicial who would be working on the budget and the details of the production.

The Genial personality is willing to sacrifice his or her own interests for the common good. They are kind and generous. They were probably class officers in high school. You'll find them volunteering their time in non-profit organizations. They want to make things better for everyone and hopefully, they'll benefit from the crumbs that fall from the table.

Ronald Reagan is a Genial who comes instantly to mind, as is Sally Jesse Raphael, Jimmy Stewart and, probably, Bill Clinton. At least in the early portion of his Presidency, Mr. Clinton found his greatest difficulty in telling people "no."

The late Audrey Hepburn would also fall into this category. She spent her last months rallying for money and food to be sent to the starving people around the world.

The strength of the Genial personality is that they're loyal to other people and they can build consensus on any subject. If they're on your team, they'll be the best glad-handers you could imagine. They're unselfish and give one hundred and ten percent.

But, their strength is also a weakness. The Genial personality can self-destruct because they bite off more than they can chew. They become over-burdened and lose their effectiveness. They can also be perceived as two-faced at times because they tend to give every person the answer they want to hear. Person A is told "yes" and an hour later, Person B is told "no" in answer to the same question. They're more concerned with keeping the peace and being liked than anything else.

We've covered three of the basic personality types — the Judicial, the Controller, and the Genial. The final quadrant is on the bottom right hand corner. These are the Talkative personalities.

They are High Force and High Conformity individuals. They're very verbal and they like to be on the fast-track. They're outgoing and ego-oriented and want to be where the action is. They like to be the center of attention. They want people to pay attention to them. The limelight is important.

I have to admit, I fall in this quadrant. As a speaker, I most enjoy being in front of people. I think it's fun to be recognized on the street by people who have heard my speeches, and I want people to like me.

A typical charismatic Talkative might be Regis Philbin from the "Regis & Kathi Lee" show. Joan Rivers would fall into this category and so would Ed McMahon and a host of other show business personalities. I use them as examples because they're easy to pick out and well-known to everyone.

The strengths of the Talkative personality are that they're charismatic, dynamic and personable. They're highly verbal.

People like them and want to be around them.

The weaknesses they have to guard against are that they can be undisciplined and disorganized — two qualities that can turn people's respect into resentment when the Talkatives don't follow through on their commitments. They are so concerned with the activity of the moment that they don't plan ahead. They expect others to pick up the pieces so they can get on with what they find more interesting.

As Talkatives, we are used to being able to talk our way into...and out of...any situation. Unfortunately, this can also mean that we have the mistaken assumption we can get by without doing our homework or paperwork.

We now have a good picture of how we function in this world of ours. The question is, what do we do with all this insight?

Well, what we have to do is be aware of the conflicts that arise when the four personality types connect with each other.

For instance, when a Judicial and a Talkative are seated at the same table, the Judicial perceives the Talkative as a phony — while the Talkative is trying to stay awake because the Judicial is so boring. At the next table, the Controller is disdainful of the Genial — who has been judged "a wimp" — while the Genial is barely tolerating the Controller who is obviously a real jerk.

You can tell how the conflicts arise between people and yet the differences between us are in our style. We each approach a situation from a different standpoint, each with our own reading on the matter.

Each of the personality types reacts to the same situation differently even though the outcome may be the same. I'll try to make this clearer for you.

Let's imagine four guys are on the first tee of the golf course. They represent the four personality types and they're in the same foursome. The Controller will tee off first so he can lead the group around the course and report on the best way to play each hole. The Genial will make sure everyone likes the look of the greens and keep reminding everyone on how gratifying it is that they can spend the day together in good company. The Judicial will be pacing off the next shot and spending a lot of time at ground level sighting down his club shaft to check for any potential problems. And, the Talkative will be giving a running commentary on how much his game has improved since his last time out — and chatting with the foursome coming up behind.

Or, let's take that same foursome into the Pro Shop. The Controller will want to buy what is needed and get on with the round. The Judicial will be examining a golf club or shirt very closely and checking for workmanship. However, the Judicial will probably wait before buying until several competitive stores have been checked out and prices compared. The Genial will be finding new products to show the rest of the group and getting enthused with the fun that could be had if they all bought the same club covers. The Talkative will be in the lounge telling stories and discussing the merits of a new putter without ever making up his mind to buy anything.

The question that comes to mind is: why would this foursome ever come together if we tend to associate with people like ourselves? Well — why do opposites attract? Simply because my weakness will be complemented by your strength.

My disorganization will be lessened by your attention to detail. Your need to keep the peace will be countered by my need to speak out on any issue. The various personalities can co-exist very well if they just understand how the inter-personal system of checks and balances can work.

Whether on a personal — or a professional — level, you have to communicate with other people in the way *they* want. Again, we're talking about the mirroring that I described yesterday.

When you know how someone else responds to a situation, then you have only to approach them in the proper manner.

What I mean by this is: if you're talking to Judicials, be thorough. When you're trying to convince Controllers, be direct. With Genials, be appreciative, and with Talkatives, be animated.

Here's an example.

Let's say you're presenting an idea to your boss. Now you know it's a good idea and you're sure it could make a significant difference in the efficiency in your department — but first you have to convince your manager.

The first action you have to take is make a Personality Action Graph so you know how your boss operates. You have to determine which quadrant he or she belongs.

If you're dealing with a Judicial, you need to make a half-hour appointment in advance and sit down with a sheaf of facts and figures. The more statistics and computer printouts and case histories that you can come up with the better.

The Judicial is like the college professor who would throw the term papers up the stairs and the one that landed on the bottom step, because it was the heaviest, got the "A." Convince your Judicial boss the same way you handled your teacher. Pad the presentation with paperwork.

If you're dealing with a Controller, then you need to walk into the office and ask for three minutes of their time. Present a quick summary of your idea, outlining the problem, the solution, and the benefits that can be realized. The whole idea could fit on one page and the Controller would be happy. Be very direct and up-front. Give the definite impression that by passing it on to this person, you know your idea is in good hands.

With the Genial boss, you might want to arrange an informal meeting. As soon as you're together, show your appreciation for the company and the leadership. Talk about the way a departmental task force could be set up to oversee this new idea and how the employees would benefit from working together. Talk about the common good and the positive ways in which this idea would have an impact on the company as a whole — and down the line, the customers.

Now, if you're dealing with a Talkative boss, you want to come on like gang-busters. You need a good deal of enthusiasm. You want to be excited and to get your boss caught up in your passion for the idea. As much as possible, give the impression that if it weren't for the outstanding leadership, you'd never have come up with this innovation. Your animation is just a pale reflection of the atmosphere that has been created in the office.

When you do this, you will find you have become very effective. Suddenly, the course of your career will begin to take a definite upswing. You've learned how to deal with people in the body language and philosophical framework that makes them comfortable.

One of the criticisms you may hear from your family, friends, and co-workers is that you've become a phony. You're no longer being yourself. You're playing up to the person in power. Don't pay any attention to them. What you're doing is communicating on the level of the person you're talking to. People on radio and television do it everyday.

Naturally, you shouldn't overdo your shifting of communication style. For instance, be more animated if you are talking with a Talkative, but there's no need to turn cartwheels. Merely pick up your enthusiasm level a bit, and you will find the Talkative will respond positively.

When I am hired to speak to a new client company, the first questions I ask are: Who are these people? What do they do? What do they want to learn today? How can I be most effective with them? The meeting planner is more than happy to answer these questions. In the best of all circumstances, they'll have sent me all the written material they have on the company. When I arrive, they give me a tour of the facility and let me talk with some of the key people. I learn the vocabulary of their industry. I know enough to tailor my remarks to their frame of reference.

Does that make me a phony? Of course not! It makes me a communicator.

For example, how popular would I be if I was talking to a group of Federal Express employees — line people who move packages from point A to point B all day long — and I used nothing but examples from the insurance underwriting business?

I might as well be speaking Greek. They'd have no idea what I was talking about — and they'd never ask me back. And, who could blame them?

What we all need to cultivate is Flexibility. Remember that from yesterday? Along with Force and Control, we need to be versatile. We have to "go with the flow."

If, when we were going through the four personality action styles, you recognized yourself in more than one style, then you're already on your way. The more you can participate in each of the styles, the more Flexible you are.

The personality styles are very much like Priorities. While one will always be dominant, there are others that are also important. In the same way, while you may be primarily a Genial, you may have some Controller and Judicial characteristics if you have a high score on Flexibility.

There may be a lot of Talkative in you even though you're primarily Judicial. Look at someone like Judge Wapner of *People's Court,* one of the most popular television shows of all time. Judge Wapner is a real judge so you know he's primarily Judicial. That's a given.

He takes facts and analyzes them before giving a decision. But he also has some Talkative personality traits. He enjoys the limelight and likes the attention he receives as a television personality.

Ross Perot is another good example. Basically, he's certainly a Controller...but he also likes to be in front of the public. There is a definite strain of Talkative in him when he consistently shows up on television, and the way he wants to unite the country for the common good is one of the traits of the Genial.

It could be argued that all his charts and graphs also show Judicial tendencies. However, if you were to approach him with a proposal, you'd want — first and foremost — to be direct. You'd have to back up your forthrightness with facts and figures, delivered in an upbeat and enthusiastic style.

If this sounds complicated, take heart. It really isn't as difficult as it seems. Like any new behavior, you need to practice. This is similar to our earlier example of changing the way you cross our arms or refolding your hands.

It's going to feel awkward and unnatural at first. That's to be expected. I suggest you practice first with your family. They are already inclined to like you and agree with you, so use them as guinea pigs.

Try out your new communicating techniques during the next family gathering. Make sure you've worked out Personality Action Graphs for each member of the group. Watch the changes in the way you interact with each one.

If young people and their parents could be taught this technique, we'd probably wipe out much teenage angst.

Kids could analyze their parents' styles and present ideas that would be received without hostility. Instead of fighting a Controller Mom, the teen would know to be direct and up front with her. Instead of being frustrated when a Judicial father says absolutely "no car," the teenagers would know that they have to present all the financial facts and figures, how they will pay for it, what the insurance premiums will be, and what the gas will cost. Combine that with how much money they're earning as a part-time clerk at the video store and the promise of good grades and I can promise you that even the most stern parent will at least give their teen a fair hearing.

After you've practiced with the family, move on to your close friends. You'll find that it won't be long before you're getting very comfortable with the process.

I never have to write down the graph anymore. After I've talked to someone for a few minutes, I can plot their personality style in my head. You'll be able to do it, too. Like the old story of the New York street musician who was asked how to get to Carnegie Hall — the answer's the same. "Practice. Just practice."

It's been shown that communication is the most vital skill we have. We don't always stop to realize that we communicate every minute of every day. If we're smiling or frowning, laughing or crying, sitting quietly or nervously pacing the floor, hurrying down the street or walking casually without much direction — these are all communication devices. Speaking and writing are actually very sophisticated ways of communicating. The point is that you need to spend as much time as necessary to learn how to communicate easily and effectively with the people who can take you closer to attaining your goal. We'll talk more about the importance of communication skills tomorrow.

And with that, we conclude Day Eleven of our Fourteen Day **Just Say Yes!** A Step Up to Success Program. So far, we've taken you from the foundation of identifying your priorities through goal setting to objectives and daily actions and started in on communication skills.

Before tomorrow, I want you to continue to work with your Personality Action Graphs. Re-evaluate some of your earlier graphs now that you have a better idea what each quadrant signifies. Practice your new communication skills with friends and family.

You've laid all the groundwork. Tomorrow, we move into the home stretch of this program. You'll take the first three of the Six Steps to Success. You're going to find this an exciting time — one that will really change how you view your present and plan for your future.

# The Six Steps Up to Success, Part One

One of the interesting comments I get about this program is that the **Just Say Yes!** process is a little like building a house. By now, you have put all the bricks and concrete and wood and plumbing and appliances and furniture in place. The house is full and it radiates success. Next, we're going to build the six steps that will take you up to the front door. These are the six steps that will bring you up to the goals you have decided are important for you.

These six steps will be continual points of reference for you. They were discovered after lengthy research in the works of the great thinkers of all times — along with a great deal of practical experience that has confirmed everything I had discovered.

Sometimes I'm told that these steps are really very simplistic and obvious. That's right! Often it's the most obvious advice that's the most ignored.

It's the story of the Acres of Diamonds all over again. In this story that the late Earl Nightingale told so well, an African farmer had one goal in life — to leave his simple home and find his fortune. Finally, he sells his land, takes the money and spends the rest of his life traveling from one end of the world to the other, searching for the elusive pot of gold. As an old man, he returns to his home and where his modest house once stood is a huge mansion. He knocks on the door and is taken to the person who had bought his farm so many years ago — only to find that acres of diamonds were discovered under his original farm. The farmer had traveled thousands of miles to look for wealth that had been under his feet since the day he was born! So, if the six steps you're going to learn appear to be obvious at first, remember that the obvious is often the most easily ignored.

You will find that these steps are also unique in that they'll work both in your personal and professional life. And, you'll find they make your life less complex and more productive in today's changing times.

Just like the example of the florist we talked about in the beginning, it is how you take these simple truths and build your own bouquet that will make them special and unique in your life.

Does this sound too good to be true? Well, don't make the mistake of thinking that because these steps are simple, they are also easy.

Think about it. Singing is easy but most of us don't do it very well. If it was all that easy, we'd all be Barbra Streisand.

Dancing is easy...but there's only one Baryshnikov.

Millions of people across America have a basketball and a hoop but there's no one quite like Michael Jordan.

Just about anyone can put words on paper, but there are very few Ernest Hemingways being published today.

The reason Ernest Hemingway and Michael Jordan and Mikhail Baryshnikov and Barbra Streisand are outstanding in their fields is because they make the difficult look so simple that we all think we can do it, too. I have often said the hardest thing in the world is to do something so well it looks easy.

When I've asked business leaders where they most often find mistakes are made, they'll tell me they "messed up on the basics." It's the basics — the simple stuff — that trips us up.

In the same way, because these six steps could be perceived as being basic and simple, it doesn't mean that they're going to be easy for you to apply in your daily actions. The whole key is going to be in your application and execution of the principles I'm going to give you.

### ⬛1️⃣ The First of the Six Steps to Success is: *Appreciate What You Possess.*

Appreciate what you possess. I don't mean this in a material way. This isn't the time to pet your Porsche — or tap your Taurus!

What I mean is you need to nurture what is vital to your life instead of being so caught up in striving for achievement. Look around you at your relationships with people you love and care about — at your talents and abilities — at your hobbies and pleasure activities — at all the elements of life that make it special for you. Take the time to stop and smell the flowers in your life.

When I look back on my childhood, I have some fabulous memories — and like most of you, some that I'd just as soon forget!

Some of the most vibrant memories are connected with the little Methodist Church that was located right in the center of Crothersville.

In 1969, I won the local speech contest sponsored by the Soil and Water Conservation Agency. The purpose of the contest was to get high school kids to be aware of the importance of ecology and conservation.

Well, that was all the Reverend Gardner needed to hear. As long as there was a prize-winning speaker in his congregation, he could go away for a weekend and "that young McKain boy" could fill in for him. How could I turn him down? — even though moving from talking about soil conservation to addressing a Methodist congregation did involve a certain leap of faith...on his part and mine.

Never in the history of the Sunday sermons did any fourteen-year-old preacher work harder on his exhortation. I was sure my sermon would go down in the church records right next to those of the founder, John Wesley.

Sunday morning arrived and it was unbearably hot and humid. I looked out over a sea of people, each stirring the air with paper fans that said "Kovernor's Funeral Home." After the opening hymns, I rose to speak. The big clock on the wall in front of me said ten o'clock and I knew that I only had twenty-five minutes to impart my wisdom before releasing the congregation for Sunday School.

I began by expressing my appreciation for the opportunity to speak to these sinners with whom I'd been attending church my entire life. I quoted the scripture that had been a comfort to me through the trials and tribulations I'd faced during the vast experience of my fourteen years.

With a deftness that impressed even me, I moved smoothly from scripture to interpretation. By using numerous "th" sounds at the end of my words, I felt I had adopted a truly religious style. I told my attentive audience that the book of First John should speak to all of us because "if a man sayeth that he loveth God but hateth his neighbor, he be-eth a liar."

I warmed up to the subject explaining, "If he can love God —
Whom he has never seen — how can he not love his neighbor who
he sees daily?"

At this point I looked directly at my playground nemesis,
Frankie Salsberry, and hoped that the magnanimous look of
brotherly love I gave him would erase our previous hostility.

Now, with a full head of steam behind me, I went for the
emotional close. I led the congregation in a big, meaningful prayer.
Sweat dripped off my body and I longed to have one of those
funeral parlor fans — but I'd done it. I'd saved souls.

Full of self-righteous pride in my morning's accomplishment,
I returned to my seat and looked at the big clock on the wall, hoping
against hope I hadn't talked too long and that I'd finished in time to
get the youngsters to Sunday School.

No problem. Big problem.

The clock on the wall said it was ten-o-four. My moment of
glory lasted about twenty-one minutes short of the time allotted. An
embarrassed silence filled our church.

To this day I'm grateful to the Sunday School Superintendent,
Leroy Senn. He stood up and looked at the bemused congregation.
He smiled and said: "I'm reminded today of how we need to be
thankful for the blessings we have around us. Scott, your message
wasn't long in duration...but it was long in feeling and effort. I
thank you for that.

"And," he continued, "I hope that we, as a church and as
individuals, never forget to take notice of, and glorify in, those
moments of life that often slip by without our attention — like when
a young person stretches to do something only previously done by
adults — or the smile of our spouse — or the laugh of our parents.

"Applause isn't usually heard in our church, but let's show
Scott our appreciation by giving him a hand."

To this day, after being applauded by thousands of audiences
around the world, I can't remember a sweeter ovation — or one that
meant as much. The congregation applauded — then rose to sing
the hymn: "Count Your Blessings — Name Them One by One."

It turned out that the summer Sunday sermon had indeed
changed the life of at least one soul in Crothersville — mine! I
learned to count my blessings.

Studies are constantly published showing that appreciation is one of the most powerful tools we have.

Motivational Research, a marketing research firm, recently reported that over one fourth of all Americans — 27.1%, to be exact — would leave their current jobs, no matter what their seniority or salary, and take another that offered more generous recognition. In other words, the money and security weren't as important as being appreciated.

Sadly, the same study reported that thirty-eight percent of American workers say they "rarely" or "never" receive praise from their superiors.

I want you to take a few minutes right now and write down what you should be happy about. Count your blessings and name them, one by one. In your notebook, list what's important to you. Don't try to be too philosophical or emotional about this process. You may want to place people, beliefs, and opportunities above everything else. Someone else may want to list material possessions along with the intangibles.

After you make your inventory, then document the ways in which you think you can enhance it. Working with your priority values, what can you do to make your life better?

Make that list. When you're done, rejoin the book, and we'll go on to Step Two.

I am not a betting man, but I would be willing to wager that as we continue through these steps, you may remember other blessings you want to include. Just jot them down as they occur to you.

For me, my wife Sheri is at the top of my appreciation list. I am so very grateful she's in my life. My parents and other members of my family are also on the list, along with friends and mentors.

I put down my ability to communicate, the computer equipment I use every day in my work and really enjoy, my home, my car, our dogs, the people who believe in me, my clients, . . . my list is really very long. When I look at it, I become more appreciative of the tangible rewards I have received in my life. I turn this appreciation into a springboard to move me closer to the accomplishment of my goals. You can do the same.

| 2 | **Step Two of the Six Steps Up to Success is:** *Communicate Effectively* |

Yesterday, we discussed the importance of communication styles and how they affect inter-personal relationships. I want this concept fully impressed upon your consciousness, because I've never met a successful person who couldn't communicate effectively.

I have previously mentioned the brilliant Stephen Hawking. He is the British physicist considered the world's expert on Black Holes. He also has Lou Gerhig's disease, amyotrophic lateral sclerosis, and he is confined to a wheelchair, unable to speak. Still, he communicates! He writes books — one laborious letter at a time. He converts his sounds and movements into speech through the translation skills of his assistants who are with him daily. He refuses to allow a physical disability to prevent him from interacting with his universe.

The same could be said for Helen Keller who was blind and deaf because of a high fever in infancy.

Today, the actress Marlee Matlin has proved that being profoundly deaf does not deter you from winning an Oscar — as she did for *Children of a Lesser God*. She can't hear — and her speech is distorted — but she is a world-class communicator.

I prepared this program at my computer and I remember what a struggle I went through to buy this equipment. At the time, my business was growing by leaps and bounds and it was time to join the Twentieth Century and enter the computer age. The challenge was that I didn't know anything about computers.

Thus unprepared, I went to Computer Store Number One. The salesperson asked me what kind of computer I wanted and I said: "Hey, I don't know anything about computers."

"Fine," I was told. "Here's a whole handful of brochures. You go and do your homework and then come back here when you know what you want and we'll talk."

This sent me to Computer Store Number Two.

Here, the salesperson was much more helpful when I admitted my lack of knowledge. "No problem," I was told. I might add here that it has been my experience that the very worst problems crop up right after I've been told, "No problem!"

The salesperson continued. "Look at this configuration. It's the Jujitsu X70. Six megabytes of RAM. 80 meg hard drive. Comes with a beautiful VGA monitor and full "scuzzy" support. It's got a really fast 486 board — and I can throw in a box of double density floppies. Shall I put it on your credit card?" I wandered out the door in a daze, wondering what language this person was speaking and how I would ever learn it.

By this time, I was seriously thinking of being a trailblazer by being the only business that was NOT converting to computer. Finally, I gave it one more shot and went to Computer Store Number Three. I was approached by a salesperson who said, "Hi, my name's Connie. What's yours?" Finally, a question I could answer!

"I'm Scott — and you're the first salesperson to ask me that."

Connie smiled. "I'm not surprised," she said, "But you'll find that we're not here just to sell computers. If you and I can communicate effectively, we can provide some solutions for your business and the computers will take care of themselves. Now, tell me about the business you're in and what you need the computer to do."

Then, Connie did something truly remarkable. She *listened* — and as I babbled on about my lack of experience and my nervousness and my needs, she continued to listen. She even took notes. What I was saying was important to her.

Anyone want to guess where I bought my computer?

The truth is that talking should represent no more than thirty-three percent of our verbal communication. Listening and understanding are, by far, the more important parts of the equation. You've heard it said, "God gave us two ears but only one mouth." That says something about how much we should listen compared to how much we talk.

I want to make an important distinction here. Hearing is a physical action. It refers to sound waves hitting the ear drum, causing it to vibrate and transmit a signal to the brain where the impulse is translated into what we hear.

Listening, on the other hand, is a function of effort. You have to work to concentrate and understand and stay focused. If the person who's talking to you isn't being understood, even the most profound truth is no better than the worst falsehood.

In the mid-1970's when I was fresh out of college, Werner Herzog heard me give a speech.  Mr. Herzog is a film director and he offered me a part in his next film, *Stroszek*.

The movie which, through no fault of mine, became an award-winner around the world,  told the story of three misfit German immigrants in the United States.   My role was as the banker who first finances their American Dream, then repossesses their mobile home.

We filmed one scene I particularly remember just outside Stevens Point, Wisconsin, in late November.  If you've ever spent any part of a winter in Wisconsin, you know how cold it was.

My one line in this scene was: "Our bank is here to auction Mr. Stroszek's slightly used home."  Shouldn't have been too much of a challenge.

Herzog wanted me to look cold, so he sent me outside a few minutes before we were to shoot so I could get properly chilled. Later, the rest of the cast and crew joined me, took their places and readied themselves for the scene.  There were only moments of daylight left so we wanted to do this in one take.

Mr. Herzog was ready.  He shouted "Action!" and all eyes turned to me.  You could read the dismay on their faces.  I was way past cold.  I was *frozen through.*  The camera panned in for the close-up and I tried to get my line out past my chattering teeth.  "Our b-b-b-bank is h-h-h-here to au-au-au-auction M-M-M-M. . . "

"CUT!"

In retrospect, I understand why Robert Redford has never considered me real competition.  (But, if Hollywood ever needs someone to play the lead in *The Mel Tillis Story...*)

After I warmed up, we filmed the scene.  This segment of the film shows that following my foreclosure on the home, I brought an auctioneer out to the lot to sell all of Stroszek's possessions.

As another character sees his belongings auctioned away, he begins a long, rambling diatribe directed at the auctioneer and me. Of course, it's all in German.

After listening to the old man rant and rave at us in a language we don't speak, the auctioneer looks at me, playing the American banker — then at the old German immigrant — and says, simply, "I'm sorry, sir.  I don't understand you."

*What a great double meaning!*

Not only didn't he understand the man because he was speaking another language — he also didn't understand him as a *person* because they were unable to communicate.

If I don't understand you as a person, I'll never be able to communicate with you effectively as an equal. This means we not only have to share a language, but I also need to know what your ethnic background, experience, values and lifestyle have brought to the mix. I have to understand where you fall on the Personality Action Graph. I have to know your vocabulary and your frame of reference.

If you're a Native-American who has always lived on a reservation in New Mexico and I'm a Maine lobster fisherman who's spent his entire life "down east," we're not going to communicate easily. The same is true if you're a New Yorker who's never been out of the concrete canyons and I was born and raised on a farm in Iowa. It will be hard to find a common ground that we can use to understand each other. When you're worrying about what the winter will do to your crops, I'm worrying about how I'm going to get cross-town in the snow.

Perhaps, the real word we should use when talking about communication is "focusing." We need to focus on what the other person is saying and understand the background from which they're saying it.

We can revisit the Golden Rule. Jim Cathcart is my good friend and one of the most honored professional speakers in the country. Jim goes beyond the Golden Rule to what he calls "the Platinum Rule" — which is, "Do unto others the way *they* want to be done unto."

We touched on this earlier but it's well worth repeating. You should treat people in a way to fulfill *their* expectations, not yours. We should communicate people in the way that they can find a commonalty with us.

How do you know what other people want?

Listen! They'll find a way to let you know. When you don't listen, you can set up an explosive situation like the riots in Los Angeles in the spring of 1992. One person after another interviewed on the streets, with buildings burning behind them, said, "We couldn't get their attention any other way. Nobody would listen." So, they destroyed part of their city in a bid to be heard.

I read somewhere, "A good listener isn't only popular everywhere, but after a while, a good listener knows something!"

With that in goal in mind, let's look at the four basic rules of listening. One, give non-verbal and verbal responses. Two, give and seek feedback. Three, maintain good eye contact. And Four, take notes and follow-up.

By saying: "give non-verbal and verbal responses," I mean you should demonstrate that the information is being received. Have you ever been talking to someone on the phone and you hear nothing but dead silence? After awhile, you begin to babble — and then you slow down — and then you finally ask, "Are you still there?" When they say "yes," don't you feel as if maybe you aren't really the center of their attention?

It's very reassuring to have the person you're speaking to respond by nodding or making some little non-committal sound — "Mmmm! . . . Really?. . . . Uh huh. . .Okay" and so forth. Let the other person know they've made contact. It's one of the first lessons that actors learn — don't just act — *re*-act.

The second rule of listening is "give and seek feedback." Show that you not only understand but are willing to give some information in return.

An occasional "I know how you feel" or "That must be very uncomfortable" or "Is there any way I can help?" shows the other person you are turned on and tuned in. Volunteer any information that you have that might help. Let the listener know you're ready and willing to cooperate with them.

The third rule of listening is to maintain eye contact. I know several people who never seem to look at me when we're talking. Their eyes are always skidding around the room, checking out who else is there and if there's anyone more important to talk to.

Now, maybe I'm being a little paranoid but I don't think my reaction is unusual. If you want to demonstrate your interest in another human being, just look at them directly while you're talking to each other. It's probably the most flattering gesture you can make.

That goes for your spouse and children as well as those you encounter in the workplace. Children want to know you care enough to put down the newspaper or turn off the television to listen to what they're concerned about. Your spouse may need someone who will be a non-judgmental sounding board — and who could be better than you? Invest a few minutes of quality time and reap an incredible harvest of love and respect.

And finally, listening rule number four — take notes and then, follow-up. Taking notes on what the other person is saying gives the sense that you consider the information important enough so you don't want to forget it. Sending a note or phoning later reinforces that impression.

To sum up the second step to success — Communicate Effectively — I ask you to make an effort to understand, because without understanding, there is no communication. Focus on others — because without an outer-directed focus, your communication is aiming in the wrong direction. And, make every effort to communicate simply and effectively — because that is one of the basic truths about success.

Tomorrow we'll talk about Steps Three and Four in the **Just Say Yes!** A Step Up to Success Program. Again, I want you to practice what you're learning. Think about your communicating skills. How can they be improved? What could you be doing that you're not doing now? How do you appear to your co-workers, your boss, your mate, your children, your parents and your friends? Do they feel that you care or that you're more concerned about yourself than about them?

Make a list in your Workbook of the steps you can take to improve your communication skills in the various areas of your life.

As you change your behavior patterns, you'll want to refer to this list. It will surprise you to find how much you've changed.

# DAY 13

# The Six Steps Up to Success, Part Two

We've talked about the first two steps leading up to our success: Appreciate What You Possess and Communicate Effectively. If you've faithfully done the exercises I've given you, you've must have seen the difference in yourself as you become more aware of how you interact with others on a daily basis.

**3** | **I told you yesterday that I'd meet you on Step Three and here I am on a step inscribed:** *Set Goals and Expect to Achieve Them.*

Let me repeat that! Set goals and *expect* to achieve them. That's right. Don't doubt yourself for even a minute.

If you are going to be successful, you've got to set goals for your life and make the specific plans you need to follow to achieve them. If you're not sure about the goals part, this is the time to go back to the chapter on Goals and rework the process until you've developed your personal blueprint for the future.

If you're still not sure why you need to do this, I recommend you re-read Lewis Carroll's children's classic, *Alice in Wonderland.*

In one part of the story, Alice is walking along and reaches a fork in the road. There, in the fork of a tree, is the Cheshire Cat.

Alice asks the Cat: "Which way do I go?" The cat responds: "Where are you going?" Alice starts to cry. "I don't know!" The Cat smiles at her wisely and says: "Then it doesn't matter which road you take."

Napoleon Hill, the author of the classic work, *Think and Grow Rich*, said: "There is one quality which one must possess to win and that is definiteness of purpose, the knowledge of what one wants, and a burning desire to possess it."

Even though we've talked about this before, I want to remind you about the properties of a correct goal. First, it must be specific. Don't set a goal of being happy or making money. Both are nice ideas but they don't have the kind of definition that every goal needs. You have to be able to touch and feel and taste your goal.

Be definite about what will make you happy — a new home, a better job, one hundred thousand dollars in savings within the next ten years and so on.

You'll find that happiness is in the process and not in the conclusion. Earl Nightingale used to give this example. "When was your family happier — on the way to the vacation destination or on the way home?" If you're like most of us, the anticipation and the travel were much more fun than the return trip after the vacation was over and you were on your way back to the daily grind. It's the journey that gives us the most pleasure — and that's why it's important to consistently set new goals as you come close to achieving your current ones. In this way, you'll continue to repeat and reinforce your successful process.

The second property of effective goals is that you must write them down. If you don't make this formal contract with yourself, you'll start to waffle when the going gets a little tough. Commit your goals to paper and read them several times a day. Under each goal, write the objectives that will make them happen — and then the daily actions that need to be taken to bring the objectives into fruition.

If you're a salesperson and your goal is to increase your sales by ten percent in the coming year, write that down. Write down the objectives that will enable you to achieve that increase. Then, in your daily planner, write down the plateaus you should have reached by certain dates. Keep your written commitment in front of you as much of the time as possible. Achieving it should have the highest priority in your plans for each day. If you don't arrange to spend a majority of your time on making this goal a reality, then you don't really have a goal, you have a dream.

I often think of that famous rallying cry of Martin Luther King, Jr. He said: "I have a dream!" I often think he really meant: "I have a goal!" *He* certainly did. He wrote about his goal. He made it very specific. He talked about it. It was something on which he spent a majority of his time during every waking moment. He even gave his life for it.

It has been said, "A goal is a dream with a deadline." I want you to set definite time lines around your goals. Know when you want them to be a reality and aim at that date. If you don't make it, set a new date and keep on trying.

The third property of a successful goal is that it's realistic. As I worked on this book, a couple in Wisconsin won over one hundred million dollars in a multi-state lottery. There's a goal. Who wouldn't want to receive almost five million dollars a year for twenty years?

But, is it a realistic goal? No, of course it isn't. Winning the lottery or hitting the jackpot in Las Vegas or inheriting several million dollars by an eccentric uncle you never met are all fun dreams — but they're not goals because they all hinge on chance. There's nothing you can do to make any one of these things happen. It's the luck of the draw and luck has no place in the goal process.

There are speakers around the country who are making big bucks by standing up in front of audiences and announcing that they haven't had a headache or a cold in fifteen years because they'd used the power of their mind to *will* the problem away. And you, they'll say with a straight face, can do the same — if you really want to.

Oh, really? Tell that to a virus!

The truth is, you do have limitations placed on you by forces beyond your control.

If you were born in Europe, moved here as an infant and are a naturalized American citizen, you'll never be the President of the United States no matter how much you believe you can. This is because the Constitution specifically says you can't. You have to be born on American soil or as the child of American citizens if you're going to occupy the big desk in the Oval Office. Henry Kissinger, for instance, who he was born and raised in Germany, can never aspire to the highest office in this land, even though he was a primary advisor to presidents.

If you're six feet tall and built like a body builder, you'll never be in the saddle of a Kentucky Derby winner. If you're five foot two and built like a soda straw, you'll probably have a tough time winning the Heavyweight Boxing Championship. There are things that just aren't realistic, no matter how much you'd like them to happen.

So when you're planning your goals, pass them through the reality check-point so you don't spin your wheels on an impossible dream instead of speeding ahead toward a realistic goal.

We live in an era of instant gratification. With the flick of the remote control, we can turn on our television and see all the problems of the world solved within thirty to sixty minutes — and that includes commercials. The media teaches us that if we have an ache or a pain, we can take a pill and pouf! — it's gone. If we have a challenge in our marriage — get a no-fault divorce. If our relationship is going sour — just walk away. If we have any other problem, no matter how bizarre, tune in Phil or Oprah or Geraldo and it'll be taken care of in no time.

In the real world, where you and I live, it is a little different. Things that really matter are going to take a little time and a whole lot of effort. We have to ask ourselves which is more important — that we reach our goal tomorrow — or that we reach our goal? So set realistic time frames and stick to them.

It's the second part of this step that deserves a lot of our attention. Set your goals and *expect to achieve them.*

The expectations phenomenon is very real and study after study  proves that it works. It's sometimes called the self-fulfilling prophecy.

One of the most famous examples of this is the teacher who received the list of her students for the new year and was delighted when she saw numerals by each child's name. Since all the numbers were above one twenty, she assumed she had an advanced class.

All year long she taught them as she felt gifted children should be taught. She expected more from them than was expected of comparable classes. Her lesson plans were more exciting than they would normally have been. The children all responded wonderfully and the grade level in that class was by far the highest in the school.

The year came to an end, and the teacher proudly received accolades not only from the parents, but from her principal and from the District Superintendent.

She was asked for her teaching "secrets." When she explained that she was only working with the remarkable I.Q. level of this particular class — as defined by the numbers next to each child's name — she noticed the principal was giving her a very strange look. "But, Ms. Jones," the principal said, "those numbers don't represent the children's I.Q. scores. They are the student's locker numbers!"

What does this prove? The teacher got what she expected from the children. Their academic prowess was nothing more than her expectation made real.

In Chicago, there is a remarkable teacher named Marva Collins. She broke away from the establishment of the school district and started her own private school in an underprivileged neighborhood. Soon, she had first grade children from the projects reading Shakespeare and Tolstoy. She made them proud to work and she expected nothing but the best from them, their parents and her other teachers. And it worked. The children learned everything Marva Collins taught them — and begged for more.

Richard Bach, the author of *Jonathon Livingston Seagull*, wrote, "Sooner or later, those who win are those who think they can." Tom Hopkins, master sales trainer, agrees. He said: "You begin by always expecting good things to happen."

Unfortunately, we humans tend to expect the worst even while we're hoping for the best. We put ourselves down even when we're reaching in new directions.

As I mentioned earlier, Dr. Robert Rosenthal called it the Pygmalion Effect. He said we consciously — and more importantly, sub-consciously — encourage what we expect will happen instead of what we want to happen. The name comes from the Greek legend in which a king, who hates women, falls in love with an ivory statue of Aphrodite, the goddess of love. Because of the King's earnest prayers to the goddess, the statue comes to life and the king marries his own creation. The legend is probably best known in its modern reincarnation as *My Fair Lady* and remains one of the most often used examples of self-fulfilling prophecy.

The exercise for Step Three is to analyze your own expectations for your goals. Look at the written commitment you've made with yourself by writing down your goals and think about how you really feel.

If your goal is to lose twenty-five pounds, do you think you will do it or are you cynical and negative? Is your self-talk defeating, reminding yourself that you never do what you say you're going to do and no diet has ever worked but you may as well give it another try — even though you doubt you'll succeed?

Or, are you affirming and positive, writing down appointments with yourself to exercise every day, cleaning out all the temptations from your refrigerator and kitchen cupboards and putting up a chart to record your progress?

If you don't expect your goals to come true, no matter what the obstacles, you'll be going uphill every step of the way.   Believe in yourself and watch the expected happen!

**4** **Success Step Number Four is a tough one:  *Work Hard!***

Ouch!  These steps would be more pleasant if we could just skip this one.  However, the truth is that you won't get anything worth having unless you're willing to work for it.

I could try to make this easy for you by saying that you can build incredible wealth, have anything you want, light a match on a bar of soap, sunbathe in Chicago in February and engage in other improbable activities without doing much more than wishing.

Sorry to disappoint you but there's no way around it.  You get what you earn.

In the 1980's, one of the clichés used most often by motivational and business authors was: "Work smarter not harder."

The reality for the 1990's and today is you're going to have to work smarter *and* harder.  The competition is tougher and the race is going to the contestant with the most endurance.  We're going to be challenged as we never have been challenged before by people who haven't been softened by our opulent lifestyle.

I remember a small-town Chamber of Commerce banquet where I was the keynote speaker.  The Chamber president talked to me at length during lunch.  "There's a lot of unemployment here, you know."  No, I didn't know.  "Yup, shops are closing because people don't have any money to buy.  Lot of bad things happening since the factory closed."  That surprised me so I asked why the factory closed.  The president shook his head sadly.

"The workers went on strike.  Plant owner said he was losing money as it was and he simply couldn't pay the workers any more. He offered profit sharing but the workers wanted a higher hourly wage.

"The owner said he wasn't in business to lose money so, when the workers wouldn't come back to work, he closed the factory before he went belly up."

I couldn't believe it. They would rather have the company close and be out of work than keep their jobs?

The president looked concerned. "That's right, Scott. The workers thought they had the upper hand and when the plant closed, they felt cheated. They think the company owed them a living and they're happy the owner lost his business. Sad thing is, they were making twenty-four dollars an hour for basically unskilled labor — and now they can't even find minimum wage jobs. Too bad."

Too bad! I think it's *tragic!*

It's a symptom of the sickness that pervades in America. We're spoiled. If the company doesn't owe us a living, then the country does. Yesterday's luxury has become today's necessity. Parents give their children stereos, color televisions, VCR's, cars and such because they don't want them so be deprived the way Mom and Dad were.

What Mom and Dad forget is that they've made it today's world because they *didn't* have everything handed to them on a silver platter. They learned the value of a dollar and the work ethic that allows you to earn it honestly.

Our friends with children are always complaining that Johnny and Susie don't appreciate all the wonderful things they've been given. I can't say much because I'm not a parent, but I remember that I was very careful with whatever I had as a child because I had to earn it. My parents believed in working for the luxuries. If I wanted a new baseball glove, then I had to earn the money to buy it. It wasn't just handed to me.

Here's a good example. Watch a baby. If you give the infant everything it cries for, it will continue to cry and it will never learn to get up on its own two feet. I watched a single mother spoil her baby outrageously. When the child was fourteen months old, he was big for his age — and still sitting down and howling whenever he didn't get what he wanted. We were at the house when Grandma came to visit from out of town. Within an hour, the child was on his feet and walking along the couch — to get the toy that his grandmother was holding just outside his reach.

Why hadn't he walked until then? He'd never had any reason to. Why do our young people seem so disdainful of everything? Maybe it's because they've never had to work for what they want.

If you want to meet someone suffering culture shock, talk to a college graduate who's about two months into their first job. They're usually stunned and amazed because the real world is a different animal than what they were lead to expect when they were in college.

Most of us in America today are like people sitting in front of a fireplace saying, "Okay, first give me some heat and then I'll give you some wood."

It doesn't work that way. I can work hard chopping wood for days on end but it isn't until my work has a goal, a direction, that anything is going to happen. Until I carry that wood into the house and put it on the log holder in the fireplace and set the kindling on fire so the log will catch, there's not going to be any heat.

My father is one of the hardest working people I've ever known. Throughout his life, he put in hours that were unbelievable. He could out-work a younger man any day. One of my earliest memories is waiting for him to come home so I could stand on the steel toes of the shoes he wore to work in the factory. Later, he was a butcher — and one of the best. Sometimes I'd go with him out to a farm. The snow would be knee-deep and we'd butcher cattle or hogs for the farmer. It was the worst kind of work imaginable but I'd watch the way the farmers looked at Dad with admiration for his precise surgical skill and I'd be so proud. The farmers knew that my father was working hard for them and they appreciated him.

Now, Dad's retired and he's not altogether satisfied with how his life has turned out. I think part of the reason for this is that he never made a plan for this later period of his life. He never felt that his efforts when he was younger were leading in a worthwhile direction.

The people in my Father's generation were taught about working hard but they weren't taught the second half of the equation. Working hard without a plan is like driving fast without a destination. You don't know where you're going even though you may be making great time!

Now, please understand, I don't want you to become a workaholic. A few years ago, I had the opportunity to spend an evening talking with Dr. Wayne Oates of Louisville, Kentucky. Dr. Oates has contributed a great deal to human understanding and one of his most significant contributions was in 1971 when he invented the word: "workaholic."

Dr. Oates told me that one of the things he discovered in workaholics was that they weren't the people who achieved the best results. While hard work is essential in any successful achievement, he said that we must also take into account the doctrine of diminishing returns. There comes a time when our effectiveness declines because we are worked out.

This self-imposed over-work has resulted in a new term — "burnout," a term that researchers have defined as being the human response to the higher levels of stress we experience in the technological world in which we live and work.

I'd take that one step further. If we assume that work is just that, something joyless that must be done, then we're going to "wear-out!"

However, if we can stretch ourselves into a new perspective, we will be able to work harder and enjoy it. The old cliché about "all work and no play makes Jack a dull boy (or Jill a dull girl)" has never been more true.

You need play time and rest time to go along with your work time. One of the dangers every entrepreneur faces is that the preoccupation with work which is the hallmark of starting up a new business doesn't continue on and on after the business is up and running.

There comes a time when even the most dedicated worker must put it all down and get away — if only for a weekend. It's difficult to accomplish that in today's world of cellular phones and voice mail and modems and faxes — but try it!

Take an afternoon and don't pick up your messages. If you don't want to go away, check into a local hotel for a night and don't tell any of your clients how to reach you. Act like a tourist in your own city.

I think that the popularity of Renaissance Fairs and Science Fiction conventions and Dungeon and Dragon games is because people are hungry to break away from the high-tech, high-powered, high stress world of the Nineties and go back to a simpler time when the pressures were so much less. The world of knights in shining armor and damsels in distress is much easier to take than the society we've evolved into with our so-called modern advances.

If you don't think we are a society on the ropes, go to California where billboards and television ads trumpet that stress on the job is a reason to claim Workman's Compensation!

I don't know about you, but I doubt I know anyone who doesn't have some stress in the office. In fact, the psychologist Peter Hansen wrote a successful book called *Stress for Success*. Dr. Hansen's premise is that without some stress, we don't work as effectively. It's that edge that keeps us alert and interested.

For your exercise on Step Four, ask yourself what you can do — and start doing right now — to work harder and smarter? What efforts are you going to have to make to reach your goal?

And, even more important, what are you going to do to reward yourself for the extra effort you're putting out? It's the little rewards along the way that make the work you put into this project so satisfying. These rewards don't have to cost much money. It can be a picnic in the park before a free summer concert or tickets to a ball game or an evening with friends. It should be something that you find fun and satisfying and it should make you feel just a little more special.

Again, it's important that you take the time and effort to write these commitments down in your Workbook. You want to be certain that you keep the promises you make to yourself and there's no better way to do that than to make that contract with yourself.

DAY
14

# The Six Steps Up to Success, Part Three

Here we are — two steps away from the doorway to your successful future. It's Day Fourteen. You have run the course and the finish line is in sight. To me, the most exciting aspect about the finish line is that it is also the beginning line — marking the spot where you start out on a bright new tomorrow.

We've talked about four of the Six Steps to Success: Appreciate What You Possess, Communicate Effectively, Set Goals and Expect to Achieve Them, and Work Hard. Today, we're going to talk about the last two steps.

## 5 | Step Number Five is: *Choose to Enjoy Yourself.*

Yesterday we talked about giving ourselves little rewards along the way to our ultimate goal. Step Number Five is a little bit different. It is concerned with your attitude along the way to your goal.

The simple truth is that success isn't worth having if you don't choose to enjoy the process of achieving it.

Most of the truly successful people who I know are having so much fun in their lives they are not able to distinguish between work and play. They approach both aspects of their lives with a zest for living and a love of what they're doing.

Think about it. If the President of the United States can go jogging every morning. . .if Ted Turner can go to a ball game. . . if John F. Kennedy found time to go sailing. . . if Malcolm Forbes had hours to spend riding his motorcycle and hot air ballooning — then you have time to have some fun.

In our society, work and play have, unfortunately, become exclusive of one another. Growing up during the Sixties, I used to hear there was a time to work and a time to play. More often than not, we worked harder now so we could play harder later. Work became the ticket to achieving several ends — only one of which was playing.

I speak at a lot of corporate functions and during these meetings, I often see the Vice President of Human Resources stand up and present a gold watch to Henry — or Henrietta — who's been with the company for forty years or more — usually in a lower level position. After the meeting, I always try to find the honoree and ask why he or she spent so many years in one place.

You'd be amazed at how many times I'm told it's because they had three or four weeks of vacation and they felt they were trapped. At their level, if they changed companies, they'd have to start all over earning that much vacation time.

To me, there's something very sad about the idea that the length of a vacation had been the major determining factor for decades of service. I'd hate to think an employee had stayed with me over the long haul only because he could then get away from me four weeks a year!

The secret, as far as I'm concerned, is to find a way to enjoy your work enough that you never feel trapped by it. That's when the "golden handcuffs" become your own satisfaction instead of the company's benefit package.

Throughout this program, I've told you that happiness is the by-product of your systematic efforts to achieve a specific goal. As you progress towards your target, you'll feel less frustrated and more contented. This will especially be true if you view the various aspects of your life as being constantly subject to change. If you don't expect any absolutes, the changes won't be so difficult to adapt to.

I was thinking about this the other day when I was on a 737 heading for California. I noticed that the pilot during this particular flight didn't take off from Indianapolis and fly straight into Los Angeles. In fact, he even announced that he had adjusted route somewhat to avoid some bumpy air. He had to make "mid-course corrections" throughout the flight for the safety and well-being of his passengers.

It strikes me that we need to view our life like a flight across country. It's not a beeline, from point A to point B. Instead, it's an ever-changing voyage that may meander off-course for one reason or another, but its destination never changes. Storm clouds might pop up along the way. We can plow right through them and ride out the turbulence or we can change direction and take a little longer to go around them. Whichever way we choose, we can enjoy the trip if we make up our minds to do so.

Perhaps, if we approach life's journey while keeping in mind that no voyage ever progresses without course correction, we can learn to enjoy the little twists and turns that can add so much spice to our existence.

I'm a real movie buff. Sheri and I see most of the films the weekend they are released. For a time, my hobby was to review movies on a local television station, and the comments were eventually syndicated to over eighty stations around the world.

One movie I reviewed that I especially enjoyed was *Parenthood*, from director Ron Howard. In the film there is a wonderful scene where Steve Martin learns that life is like a roller coaster. You can either close your eyes and hang on, hoping the ride will end safely, or you can throw your head back, laugh and enjoy yourself.

Not long after I saw the movie, I was at an amusement park and I took the time to watch people on the roller coaster. Just like the movie — some entered the car with a grim face and white knuckles. They didn't want to be there but they couldn't let the kids — or their date — go alone. The amusement park ride was just another of life's ordeals to be endured.

Other people were giggling and squirming in anticipation. They couldn't wait for their turn. They had the laughter and enthusiasm of children and you just knew they got a kick out of living. It's a sad irony that when we're adults and can most enjoy fun, we lose our ability to laugh and be childlike.

As children we were allowed — encouraged even — to run and laugh and play. As adults, we have our image to protect and if we're having too much fun, we're afraid we won't be perceived as professional. The grimness with which we face life is a tribute to the seriousness with which we view the mess of our human existence. Isn't that ridiculous?

I read a study, conducted at the University of California at Santa Barbara, in which researchers found children laugh ten times more frequently than adults. Children are probably ten times less stressed than adults, too. Don't you think there might be a correlation there?

The late Norman Cousins proved the ability of laughter to heal us when he was diagnosed with a fatal illness. He removed himself from the hospital. Set up his hospital bed in a hotel and ordered nurses with him around the clock. He also ordered every funny movie and television and radio program he could think of brought in and for the next several weeks, he watched and laughed and got better. He didn't die until some thirty years later of a totally different condition.

We've been together long enough now that I can just hear some of you saying: "Scott, you don't understand how serious my life really is. If you'd gone through all that I've gone through, you'd be serious, too." I have a friend whose widowed mother will never admit to having any fun since her husband died. "I just can't laugh anymore," she'll say plaintively. That's too bad because if her husband were alive, he'd be laughing. That's how he's most often remembered is for his great sense of humor.

Mark Twain said it: "Martyrdom covers a multitude of sins" and too often we assume the martyr pose so we don't have to stop our own private pity party and get on with life.

When you think there's nothing you can do to be happy, remember this line from a book by Dr. Alan Loy McGinnis. "Pain is inevitable but misery is optional." What a powerful message. "Pain is inevitable but misery is optional." We make our own choices in this life — whole series of choices consciously and subconsciously — and it's up to us to put the enjoyment and humor back in our lives, no matter how difficult times have become.

There are two tips I'd like to give you that I think will help you make your life more enjoyable.

First, if you can't stand your job, start today planning how to find something you do enjoy doing. Life is too short to spend your time in an occupation you hate. We only get one time around on this ride and why waste a minute being miserable over something we can change?

And second, develop a sense of balance. If the grass is greener on the other side of the street, it may not be the location. It may be that the fellow over there is tending his lawn better than you are — so don't jump ship until you've tried to make it better in your own backyard.

There's probably a pretty good reason why you're doing what you do. Don't just throw away the equity you've built up. Give yourself a chance to use these simple truths to turn your current situation in to a more positive one.

Don't be like the man with the acres of diamonds who sold the land so he could go somewhere else and look for his fortune. You may be standing in your personal pot of gold but you're so busy looking for the elusive end of the rainbow that you don't realize you've already found it.

Your exercise for Step Number Five — Choose to Enjoy Yourself — is to set an objective to find something funny about every day you live. Ask your co-workers and family to do it, too. In staff meetings — or around the dinner table — start the conversation by asking for each person to contribute a funny moment.

This is important: We're not looking for the latest joke here. We're not trying to catch up on the best from last night's monologue. This has to be an honest and true event. That's the only way this exercise will have professional value. It's also the only way that you will begin to see the natural humor that occurs in everyday life all around you.

I also want you to set aside a part of your workbook — or better yet, get some three-by-five index cards — and whenever you hear something that's humorous, write it down. Then at the stressful times, flip through your cards and chuckle a little bit.

Finally, I want you to promise yourself you'll make a conscious effort to have more fun.

Constantly ask yourself: "What can I do to make this activity more enjoyable?" This will be a tough one for you executive types who pride yourself on "not working to make friends but only working to get the job done." However, you might remember that management consultants agree: a happy worker is a more productive worker. Doesn't it follow that if you find ways to keep your people happy, they'll increase their output and you'll be perceived as a better boss?

Choosing to enjoy yourself may sound like a trivial assignment, but when it's integrated with the other five steps to success, it becomes a powerful leverage tool. Just think, if achievement isn't fun, why work so hard for it?

And now, the sixth and final step to success. I feel as if I should have a trumpet fanfare!

**6** Again, the sixth step is a simple truth you've heard many times: *Continue to Learn.*

If you don't, no matter how much you achieve and how much experience you've gained, the pathway to your success is blocked.

While I was growing up, I had the opportunity to spend a good amount of time with my grandfather. He would hand down to me these wonderful little sayings that I always thought were corny beyond belief. For example, we'd stand looking at the vegetable garden and he'd say:

"You know, Scott, life is a lot like this garden. When you're green, you're growing. When you're ripe, you've started to rot." Sure, Grandpa.

Another line I remember hearing so often was: "Never forget — it's what you've learned after you know it all that counts." Being about seventeen at the time — and definitely knowing it all — I didn't pay much attention to that line either. Today, however, I realize how right he was. If you don't continue to advance your knowledge base, you risk becoming obsolete in today's society.

We live in the age of specialization and this becomes more significant every day. The brain surgeon will be paid better than the family practitioner. The investment banker is more highly esteemed than the teller. The attorney who specializes in foreign trade or tax law will realize greater financial rewards than the lawyer who only handles divorces and wills.

Please don't misunderstand me. I'm not implying that one is better or more intelligent than the other. The professional athlete makes more than the inner city high school teacher, but I'd vote for the educator as being the more important to our way of life. All I'm saying is that society awards higher pay for perceived areas of specialization or skill. We will spend more for someone we think has a deeper pocket of knowledge. That's why independent consultants are much better paid than staff employees doing the same work.

There are three factors that determine whether or not you're a professional in your field. Number One, the professional gets paid for what they do. Number Two, your industry or business has — either formally or informally — a code of ethics that determines what is acceptable professional behavior and it has a specialized field of knowledge peculiar to it. So far, I can see you nodding your head. You know this.

However, the third factor that indicates a professional has been known to take some people by surprise. A professional has an on-going program of continuing education.

The Harvard Business School says that if you don't re-educate yourself every seven years, you'll become obsolete. I'll wager that if you're successful in your business, you have trade magazines that you read every month and meetings you attend on a regular basis.

I counsel my seminar attendees that if you want to continue to learn and develop your knowledge base, the first step you need to take is get your attitude right. When we graduate from college, we take that applause to mean the show is over. We can put away the schoolbooks and get on with "the good stuff." However, we call that final school ceremony "commencement" — which means, "beginning." Every school diploma ought to carry these six words. "Congratulations — now comes the hard part." When you leave school, that's when you begin to learn what you think you already know.

The second way to continue your education is to plan a program of learning. All the information you'll ever need is right there for the taking. Schedule yourself into seminars and extension courses. Listen to speakers. Read books and buy audio cassettes.

Join the professional associations that will bring you in contact with others in your field. In other words, become your own Professor of Achievement and Growth. As both teacher and student, you get to plan the curriculum and make sure you enroll and do the classwork.

And finally, read and read and then, read some more. Many motivational speakers will tell you that you shouldn't read newspapers because you fill your mind with negative thoughts. Poppycock! If you don't read two newspapers every day — along with Newsweek or Time every week — you're going to be floundering because you're so out of touch with the world you work in.

I started this practice in the late 1970's, and it didn't take more than a few days before it began to pay off. I found I could converse with people more easily and I could plan speeches more intelligently. I knew what was going on. It's hard to be a good conversationalist if you don't have anything besides yourself to talk about!

Continued learning — just like goal setting — is a very specific effort. You have to keep your antenna up so you can receive those wonderful little lessons in life that happen unexpectedly. Become your own university and constantly adjust your intellectual course just the way that 737 pilot corrected his navigational course.

Now you know the six simple steps to success. The truth is that each of them is important but they work best when they are being put to use at the same time.

# Conclusion

■ ■ ■

I can't believe our fourteen days together are almost over. I do hope you will re-read this book several times over the next few months so you can burn their messages into your subconscious mind and make the actions you need to take part of your conscious plan.

You want to internalize these principles so they become habits. The best gift you could give yourself right now is to go to your day planner and set aside an hour each day for the next two weeks to re-read a chapter a day and re-work the assignments. I feel this is an essential component in your plan to implement continued learning and growth.

Nevertheless, you *have* completed the **Just Say Yes!** Program. Now you're ready for the hard part — applying everything you've learned in the different arenas of your life.

Today our civilization seems focused upon self-help. There are entire sections in bookstores devoted to the subject. Seminar companies focus on self-improvement to the exclusion of everything else. Audio and video tape publishers bombard us with catalogs filled with products to help us be better than we are.

Despite this, America is one of the most violent, narcotic-addicted, and uneducated cultures in the world. Judging from the crime statistics, medical prescriptions and school test scores, all this self-help isn't helping very much.

Why?

I think it's partly the fault of the so-called "self-help experts" and partly the fault of those of us who hear but don't listen...who read but don't understand.

I have reviewed a number of self-help products over the years and I found that there's a lot of confusing advice being handed out.

Experts have conflicting opinions. That makes it very tough when you don't know who's right and who's just tearing up the scenery. Many of the ideas espoused over the last seventy years are now outdated. The authors may have been writing for a different time when people had different goals and different opportunities for achieving them.

I also think that as students, we are guilty of taking too little time to evaluate ourselves — or we arrive at a self-analysis that's so colored by our misconceptions that it's highly inaccurate. We misdiagnose the problem that we need to solve or the situation we want to improve.

This makes it almost impossible for us to apply the broadly written advice to our individual situations — so we don't do anything. We're stopped dead in our tracks. Maybe the suggestions offered in some of those programs violates our sense of ethics, values or priorities. Maybe the solution appears harder than the problem. Maybe we're so afraid we'll fail that we never even try.

But, this program is different. That's my personal guarantee to you. You know how to isolate your priorities — set your goals — list your objectives — use your time-planning to accomplish your daily activities — identify the personality types you deal with and walk up the six simple steps to success: *Appreciate What You Possess, Communicate Effectively, Set Goals and Expect to Achieve Them, Work Hard, Enjoy Yourself, and Continue to Learn.*

You now possess a complete set of keys that will unlock any door you choose to open to the future.

It won't happen overnight.

Nothing really meaningful ever does. The more valuable and precious your goal is to you, the more difficult it will seem to be to attain.

Don't give up.

And, if you ever feel you want to throw in the towel and go back to your old, unproductive, unfulfilling ways, just read a couple more stories about some people I have had the opportunity to meet.

There was the high school basketball player I used to watch back home. He was a skinny kid with a great court sense, but he went on to college and was so overwhelmed by the experience that he quit, returned to his family and worked on a garbage truck.

It wasn't long before he realized he had to pursue his dream or his life wouldn't mean very much. So he enrolled in a smaller college and took their team to the final game of the NCAA tournament. You may have heard of him — his name is Larry Bird.

Don't forget the long-haired kid I grew up with I mentioned earlier. His dad got him a job with the phone company so he'd grow up and stop spending all his time singing with rock bands. His grandmother kept a scrapbook — only it was mostly about me. Every time I'd win a speech contest or my name would be in the local paper for some reason, she'd clip it out and paste it in the book. She kept trying to tell her grandson that if he'd just be a little more like that "nice Scott McKain," he'd succeed. Her grandson — John Cougar Mellencamp — decided he would chart his own course. I wonder what *he's* doing now?

Then there was the smart-aleck host of "Clover Power," a television show about rural youth of the Hoosier state on an Indianapolis station. Because I was state president of the Future Farmers of America, I made a good guest for the viewers.

One day, this guy packed everything he owned in his pick-up and moved to Los Angeles to pursue his dream. He starved for a long time until America discovered David Letterman.

What do Larry Bird, John Mellencamp, and David Letterman have to do with this? I'll tell you — meeting them and watching them before they became successful helped me to formulate many of the principles I've taught you over the past two weeks. They used every tool you now have in *your* hands. They personify the success of prioritizing, goal setting and the six steps.

These rules work! They take time and you will get discouraged. You'll think that everyone else is lucky and you can't get a break — but you've got a written contract with yourself so you'll give it one more day.

Then, something amazing will happen.

You'll begin to see tiny portions of your dream coming true. You'll begin to  realize that you can build a great achievement on your small success.  You'll find that others think *you*'re the lucky one.

And, you'll take pride in the knowledge that you did it yourself with the **Just Say Yes!** A Step Up to Success process.  You will find that gradually — slowly but surely — you are beginning to  win. That's the very top step — and the most basic, simple truth of all.

The process works!

Define your destination and enjoy your journey.

■   ■   ■

Scott McKain presents dynamic programs on personal and professional development, communication, leadership and customer service to companies and associations across the country and around the world.

If your organization would like to bring Scott's message and merriment to an upcoming meeting, contact your favorite speakers bureau, or:

**National Coordinator**
**McKain Performance Group**
**P.O. Box 24800**
**Indianapolis, IN 46224**
**800/297-5844**

We would love to hear your comments about this book. Please contact us with your successes, challenges and achievements. In addition, if you would like information about Scott's future books and/or his audio and video programs, we would be delighted to place you on our mailing list. Simply write us at the address listed above and we will forward information to you right away.

Thank you for reading this book.
And, remember to **Just Say Yes!**